P9-CME-393

Journeys
in Legalism
& Grace

STEFAN ULSTEIN

InterVarsity Press
Downers Grove, Illinois

InterVarsity Press® is the book-publishing division of InterVarsity Christian Fellowship®, a student movement active on campus at hundreds of universities, colleges and schools of nursing in the United States of America, and a member movement of the International Fellowship of Evangelical Students. For information about local and regional activities, write Public Relations Dept., InterVarsity Christian Fellowship, 6400 Schroeder Rd., P.O. Box 7895, Madison, WI 53707-7895.

Cover photograph: Kathy Lay Burrows

ISBN 0-8308-1618-6

Printed in the United States of America

Library of Congress Cataloging-in-Publication Data

Ulstein, Stefan.
Growing up fundamentalist: journeys in legalism & grace/Stefan Ulstein.
p. cm.
ISBN 0-8308-1618-6 (pbk.: alk. paper)
1. Fundamentalist churches—Biography. 2. Fundamentalism—Controversial literature. I. Title.
BX7800.F868A43 1995
277.3'082'0922—dc20
[B] *95-25284*
CIP

20 19 18 17 16 15 14 13 12 11 10 9 8 7 6 5 4 3 2 1
12 11 10 09 08 07 06 05 04 03 02 01 00 99 98 97 96 95

For Jeanne, who led me to Christ,
and has walked with me along the way

Acknowledgments

I am deeply grateful to the scores of people who shared the joys and pains of their spiritual lives with me as I conducted interviews for this book. I began with more than one hundred interviews and chose the twenty-two that fill these pages in the hope that they would represent some of the core issues that so many ex-fundamentalists struggle with. Many of my subjects would gladly have gone on the record, while others feared that doing so would cause further damage in already-strained family relationships. Thus I chose to keep all interviews confidential for the sake of continuity.

George Marsden's *Fundamentalism and American Culture,* a balanced, compassionate and highly readable academic treatment of the fundamentalist culture, helped me to frame my interview questions and put the responses in context. Additional help in understanding the theological and historical roots of fundamentalism came from the Reverend Richard Jones. Rodney Clapp, my editor, helped me to focus the book and move it along its way to publication.

I thank my family for allowing me to spend time on this project. My wife, Jeanne, and my sons, Kenji and Tor, were, as always, helpful, understanding and encouraging. Special thanks go to Jan Ulstein and Martie Weston for unflagging moral support.

Preface: Fundamentalism Defined

The term *fundamentalism* is bandied about so indiscriminately that it is pointless to use it without qualification. For the purposes of this book, it will refer to the theologically conservative form of North American Christianity that exists within evangelical, Pentecostal and some mainline churches. The core fundamentalist doctrines include the inerrancy of Scripture, the imminent physical return of Christ, the rapture of the saints, the seven-year tribulation followed by a thousand-year reign of Christ on earth, the virgin birth, the historicity of biblical miracles and the absolute necessity of a personal commitment to Christ as a prerequisite to salvation.

The Fundamentalist Culture

But fundamentalism is more than a theological movement. It is a subculture with a complete value system that encompasses aesthetics, education and politics. The fundamentalism that white baby boomers grew up with during the fifties and sixties was concerned with biblical inerrancy, personal piety and the imminent, physical return of Christ, but it was also on the right end of the political continuum. It was distrustful of government, yet it was strongly, almost unquestioningly, patriotic. It equated America with the kingdom of God, yet preached the wickedness of society. Communism and "creeping socialism" were aligned with the forces of darkness.

As small children, the boomers watched breathlessly as Sunday-school teachers presented Bible stories on the flannelgraph. They earned points for memorizing Scripture verses and bringing their Bibles with them every Sunday, and more points for bringing unsaved friends.

At summer camp the boomers recommitted their lives to Christ before returning to the worldly snares of the public schools. At Sunday-evening services, with every head bowed and every eye closed, they were exhorted to accept Christ, or recommit to him if they had backslidden.

"Yes . . . I see that hand. God bless you. So many hands tonight. Praise God." Often the service concluded with an altar call, accompanied by the strains of "Just As I Am."

Fundamentalist churches preached the good news of Jesus Christ, along with anticommunism and a fear of intellectualism, modernism and humanism. Young fundamentalists were to be in the world but not of the world. Among the forbidden pleasures of the world were smoking (unless they lived in a tobacco-growing state), drinking and movies. Rock 'n' roll was the devil's music, and white kids were warned about the allure of the jungle rhythms that some pastors denounced from their pulpits as "nigger be-bop." Dancing was a vertical expression of a horizontal activity.

In these churches the sixties generation gap often became a gaping chasm. A generation of children was groomed to be more educated, more affluent, more happy than their parents, and to do great things for the Lord.

The boomers' parents were sacrificers who had survived the bleak poverty of the Great Depression and gone on to win World War II. They were a hardworking generation of tradespeople, factory workers, farmers and homemakers. In many cases the boomers' grandparents were immigrants who had fled the economic and social stultification of imperial Europe or Asia.

The adult generation's spiritual agenda was inextricably mingled with the desire to achieve financial security and to remain ethnically, or at least racially, pure. Jesus was the truth. They knew Jesus, so they knew the truth. Jesus wanted boys and girls to be politically conservative, fulfill military duties if called and marry within their race. He liked short hair on boys and long skirts on girls. This was the way it had been since Jesus walked the earth with his disciples. Or so the boomers were led to believe.

Where It All Began

It is helpful to look at the origins of fundamentalism, which reveal that it is really a twentieth-century American movement rather than an unbroken line of thinking that began with the apostles. Fundamentalism, like all "isms," originated in a specific place as a reaction against other isms, most notably the German higher criticism that led to various forms of theological relativism and modernism.

After the Revolutionary War and through the Great Awakening and the turn of the twentieth century, a coalition of evangelical churches served as guardians and arbiters of public morality and Christian orthodoxy. The American evangelical establishment believed that God's kingdom would be prepared before the return of Christ and that American evangelical values were an integral part of his plan. The victory of the Union in the Civil War and America's economic ascent were seen as proof of heavenly favor.

But as the evangelicals became more wealthy and educated, they fell under the influence of modernist thinking that seemed, to some of their brethren, to be chipping away at the foundations of the faith. Modernism, particularly German higher criticism's attempt to reconcile contemporary science with the Bible, was regarded as a wolf in sheep's clothing.

In 1910 Lyman Stewart, an oil magnate from southern California, commissioned a select group of Bible teachers and evangelists to pen a response to the modernist influence within the evangelical coalition. The result was a series of twelve paperback volumes, known collectively as The Fundamentals. The term *fundamentalist* was coined in

1920 to describe the conservative opponents of modernism.

Fundamentalism came on strong, but within a few years it was marginalized in American society, written off as the fading remnant of an old and discredited worldview. Its battles for pure doctrine were seen as irrelevant to an ever more enlightened age, where humankind was increasingly the measure of all things. Just as the fundamentalists had feared, many liberal congregations began drifting away from orthodox doctrines into the murky regions of psychology, sociology and modern political movements.

In recent times evangelical churches have focused on family values, therapy and lifestyle issues, but at the beginning of the century they were much more concerned with pure doctrine. While the current trend is toward independent or pandenominational megachurches, the differences between denominations in 1910 were more pronounced than they are today. Friends and business associates would debate the relative merits of Calvinism and Arminianism.

Surprisingly, the early fundamentalists were willing to compromise to include members from numerous theological traditions in their coalition. The Reformed movement was strongest, and premillennialism and dispensationalism, which later came to dominate fundamentalism, were played down because of their "controversial" nature.

While European theologians promoted modernist views of Scripture, new religions popped up in North America like dandelions on a fresh lawn. Several volumes of The Fundamentals argued against modernist movements such as Mormonism, Christian Science and spiritualism.

Almost all of the revisionists called themselves Christians, and that was a key concern of the fundamentalists. Even now many people of goodwill call themselves Christian when they really mean to say that they are nice or honest, or simply not Jewish. Modern Christians are uninformed about the theological battles that hammered out the distinctions between heresy and orthodoxy over the past two millennia. They are also unable to articulate the faith, except in sentimental terms. This is exactly what the fundamentalists feared.

When a word loses its specific meaning, it loses all meaning. The fundamentalists understood that a Christian is not merely someone who attends meetings in a church, or a nice person, or someone who is not Jewish or Muslim. The fundamentalists sought to define the terms. Those on one side of the fence would be Christians, and while those on the other side could be liberals, modernists, humanists or whatever, they would not be permitted to confuse potential converts or faithful believers by calling themselves and their new-fangled ideas Christian.

The early fundamentalists stressed evangelism and personal piety rather than social issues or politics. The Fundamentals briefly mentioned the dangers of communism and anarchy, but socialism was considered compatible with fundamentalist beliefs. The fundamentalists saw their movement primarily as a reaction against heresy.

The Evolution of a Movement

But no ism can resist change. Over the years fundamentalism took on more and more associations, and many of them were negative. Because some who called themselves fundamentalists were really just traditionalists, the term came to mean "old-fashioned" or even "backward."

The fundamentalists' quarrel with modern science was originally over higher criticism of Scripture and the diminishment of God as Creator and Sustainer. They argued that modern science was contaminated because, from their point of view, the researcher framed a hypothesis and then set out to prove it. Darwin's theory of evolution, they reasoned, was intended to prove that God was not sovereign; therefore his science was corrupted by presupposition. The Scopes Trial of the 1920s forever associated fundamentalism with an anti-science, anti-intellectual bias. Furthermore, fundamentalists' campaigns for censorship of modern art and literature that they deemed immoral gave them an aura of philistinism that further contributed to their reputation as a nineteenth-century movement discontented with progress.

Southern defenders of Jim Crow laws often invoked old-time religion in the defense of segregation. In the fifties and sixties church-basement schools were set up to avoid racial integration, adding to the sense that fundamentalism was not only backward but also racist—particularly toward African-Americans. Some fundamentalist colleges even refused to enroll nonwhite students.

Strict dress codes emerged, forbidding pants for women and fabricating "biblical" skirt-length formulas. One fundamentalist Bible college banned polka-dot dresses lest a dot appear "in a suggestive place." Likewise, patent leather shoes were forbidden for fear that boys might see the reflection of a girl's underpants. Such uncompromising regulations made fundamentalism seem prudish and antisex.

Jerry Falwell, a self-described fundamentalist, further broadened the scope of fundamentalist values in the early days of his Moral Majority, when support for the Peacekeeper nuclear missile was part of a checklist for "moral" candidates. Falwell insisted that the Moral Majority was a political organization, not a religious one. But in the public mind it was fundamentalist, even though it included large numbers of charismatics, Roman Catholics and Mormons—faiths technically considered apostate by theological fundamentalists.

As the term *fundamentalist* evolved in the public mind to mean anything reactionary or old-fashioned, its usage expanded to describe non-American, non-Christian groups. For example, the news media have appropriated the term to describe traditionalist Muslims seeking to overthrow secular governments in the Middle East. It is also coming into popular usage for Hindu traditionalists in Sri Lanka and India, and is increasingly being used to connote religious terrorism. The 1994 murder of a doctor by a militant antiabortionist and wife beater did little to dispel this notion.

For the baby boomers who came of age in the fifties and sixties, fundamentalism muddied the waters of the spiritual quest. As in any age, old ways were challenged by new ones, and fundamentalism became more and more concerned with maintaining the status quo. Young people who desired to conform to Christ were handed a long checklist of social, political and aesthetic ideals to which they also had to conform. Their spiritual venture was like one of those Senate bills that are vetoed for all the tacked-on amendments that have nothing to do with the bill's original intent.

Evangelical African-American Christians protesting institutional racism found allies among liberal white Christians and progressive Jews, while the majority of white fundamentalists and many evangelicals linked integration with modernism. Instead of joining with black Christians seeking justice from an oppressive system, fundamentalists championed segregation as part of God's plan.

Often fundamentalist leaders' public pronouncements landed them in the camp of the race-baiters. Martin Luther King Jr. was called "Martin Luther Coon" by the Klan, and the president of a major fundamentalist college in the South referred to him as "Martin Lucifer King." That drew laughs in fundamentalist circles, but not in the pages of the national newspapers. The college president complained bitterly when he later found himself referred to in the press as a "funnymentalist." Upon hearing a rumor that civil rights advocates wanted to integrate his school, he applied for a federal machine-gun permit.

The infamous Doctrine of Ham, the notion that God cursed blacks to be the perpetual servants of whites, caused many college students to write off Christianity as a haven for half-baked exegesis and folklore-as-doctrine gibberish.

Then came Vietnam. American military leaders who had fought with brilliance and valor to defeat the evils of Imperial Japan and Nazi Germany stumbled headlong into a country whose history and aspirations they did not understand. Many American servicemen, myself included, were appalled by the racist language used to defend the war. All Asians, including our allies, were "gooks," "slopes" and "dinks." Fundamentalist churches were either silent or complicit in this line of thinking. When the young people being drafted to fight this war-without-a-plan balked, fundamentalism allied itself, as it had during the McCarthy witch hunts, with America the Righteous. The American flag was regularly saluted in worship services. To protest the war was to protest America and to reject God.

Conflict Between Generations

As children of the Depression who had never finished high school sent their children off to universities in unprecedented numbers, an enormous generational chasm grew wider. Baby boomers validated the definition of a college sophomore (*soph-* is from the Greek word for "wisdom," and *-more* is from the same Greek root as "moron"): this army of wise fools challenged every value their parents had sacrificed for. In spite of the baby boomers' assets, we were an ungrateful, arrogant generation of children.

But as those who have raised children know, wise fools need loving correction. Unfortunately, many fundamentalist parents used God as a club to enforce their own preferences and prejudices. Too many white baby boomers read Gandhi and Thoreau in college and then heard their Christian elders disparage Martin Luther King Jr. as the "head nigger in charge." Blacks, who could finally go to the good schools with white kids, found chilly receptions at the doors of their white friends' churches.

Science students examined the fossil record while their fundamentalist pastors and parents mocked whole academic disciplines. Geology, archaeology, biology and astronomy were denounced *in toto* as smoke and mirrors. I recall one well-meaning deacon in 1968 "proving" from some biblical text that human beings would never set foot on the moon. The end times were here, he announced, and the rapture would occur before the Apollo capsule could ever set down on the lunar landscape.

The political and academic gap caused boomers to question everything their parents had taught them. If their elders were so wrong about race, the war and science, then maybe they were just as wrong in the area of personal morality.

The sexual revolution encouraged young people to enjoy guiltless, recreational sex—made possible by the twin safety nets of birth control and antibiotics. The churches preached virginity followed by a life of devoted monogamy, but by the sixties and seventies the boomers' parents were divorcing in record numbers. Among those who did stay married, there were too many gloomy unions "for the children's sake," which made a hollow mockery of Christian marriage. The choices seemed to be eros and freedom versus responsibility and self-denial.

Fundamentalism also clashed with feminism, forcing more young Christians to choose between their faith and their sense of what was right. Women sought equal pay for equal work, and some claimed the right to choose not only birth control but also abortion. Feminists challenged the notion that a man could beat or rape his wife with legal impunity. Fundamentalism aligned itself against feminism in the name of God's plan for male headship of the family. Victims of abusive fathers found themselves having to choose between their Christian faith and the feminists who championed their quest for justice. It was "us or them," with no in-betweens and no sorting out of the issues.

As the dark secrets of childhood sexual abuse entered the public discourse, too many respected churchmen were revealed as pedophiles and pederasts. Many young adults who came forward for healing and justice were further humiliated by a patriarchal structure that stressed obedience to authority and silence for the sake of the church's reputation. Churches struggled to keep their secrets and their leaders' prerogatives rather than seeking justice for their children. The millstone might have been a good replacement for the necktie in many congregations.

In the Aftermath

If the fundamentalist experience had been all negative, it would not be an issue for so many of today's baby boomers. But it was *not* all negative. Those fundamentalist churches, despite their many flaws, preached the gospel of Jesus Christ. They taught young people to read the Bible and take it seriously. True, they were blinded by the Zeitgeist (and often willingly), but so was the rest of society.

The nagging problem that so many ex-fundamentalists face is that they cannot escape the legacy of their upbringing. They long for the sense of belonging brought about by the Christian fellowship and bonding that they experienced as children. They miss the warm assurances of a world with clearly defined right and wrong. They want it for their own children. But they do not want the guilt, shame and self-righteous arrogance that came along with it. They do not want to set themselves against their children and society by taking an intractable stand on every issue only to discover later that they were wrong. Unlike their elders, who grew up with a sense of knowable truth, the boomers wrestle with multiple ambiguities. Their worldview stresses pragmatic solutions and emotional well-being. They eschew battles over dogma and doctrine and long for a community of believers who can be identified by their love for one another.

Some have remained fundamentalist, but even they have abandoned many of the "truths" they learned as children. Others have moved on to churches that hold fast to Christian orthodoxy without the fortress mentality that had set them against science, art and literature. Many have embraced New Age philosophies and Eastern religions.

A great number languish in spiritual limbo, unable to commit themselves to Christ yet unsatisfied by the trendy hodgepodge of New Age and humanistic psychobabble that is the current replacement for faith. They wander, like Hamlet's father, unable to find a resting place.

Listening to Ex-fundamentalists

This book is an attempt to give a public hearing to ex-fundamentalists. I have tried to avoid steering the interviews toward any predetermined conclusions. No two stories are identical, but the reader will probably see common threads woven throughout the narratives.

I hope that this book will be helpful to those still struggling with the heritage of their fundamentalist past. We often learn from the stories of others what we cannot learn on our own.

Perhaps parents of estranged baby boomers will find some help here too. It is hard for children to talk about the past with their parents. Too often we bite our tongues and go home angry, or descend into accusation and recrimination. I hope that the distance of anonymity will allow parents to hear from others what they cannot hear from their own children. It is my deepest desire that every reader will be drawn closer to Jesus Christ by reading these stories.

I have not attempted to sort out the doctrines or history of fundamentalism with academic precision. Rather, I have tried to examine the fundamentalist experience on a personal level. Few people come to Christ for pure doctrine, and few leave the church over theological abstractions. Our place in the body of Christ is usually guided by the way people around us live their lives and by the ways that they help or hinder us in our own journey. The role of the church is not to prove itself right at the expense of human relationships but to become more Christlike.

Part 1

Life in the Church: The Separated Life Revisited

1

Our Sense of Right Can Close Us Off from Others

As an administrator at a Christian college, he meets students from a wide variety of evangelical backgrounds. He often counsels students who, like himself, struggle to reconcile a fundamentalist worldview with modern academia.

We meet for lunch on the campus and eat in an open area under century-old oaks whose early-summer foliage provides a lush emerald canopy. Tanned students in shorts and summer dresses stroll languidly on the paths or sit beneath the trees chatting with friends.

He seems to fit this environment. His quick wit and self-effacing humor are balanced by a sense of spiritual and intellectual longing in his voice. His warm eyes are windows to a soul that yearns for a deeper union with God and his fellow human beings.

As we begin, I sense that he has covered this ground before, and that impression is confirmed as we talk. His life and his faith are one, and he is quick to point out that he was introduced to Christ by the fundamentalist church of his youth, a church from which he is now somewhat estranged.

* * *

What I appreciated about the fundamentalist church I grew up in was the desire to take Scripture seriously. That was always the most important thing. But it's also what I found to be the most detrimental as I grew older. There was so much baggage in the ways we were taught to interpret the Scriptures that I needed to be around some nonfundy types to get clear of that baggage.

As a kid I read Scripture verses, memorized them and pondered them. I took my Bible to services and followed along, but I was troubled by this nagging inner voice that said, *What you're seeing in Scripture is different from what you're seeing in church. There is something about Jesus Christ in the Gospels that is different from the Jesus Christ we talk about.*

Can you put your finger on what that difference was?

We read parables that Jesus told and interpreted them legalistically. A fair reading of the parables requires you to be nondidactic. In our church they were interpreted without grace.

As a kid I was never taught about the origins of fundamentalist tradition. Something about the way it was presented implied longevity, as though it was as old as the apostles. But really, in the sixties fundamentalism was only forty or fifty years old. I suppose that the early 1920s, when fundamentalism took root, would have seemed as distant to me as the Reformation, but I was given no sense of a historical timeline. The only thing that was important in our training was what current fundamentalist ideologues were saying.

My first breakthrough came in a college class on the wisdom literature of the Bible. The professor wouldn't let us say what we had learned in church. He made us read the Scriptures and deal with what they actually said. For some people it was terribly threatening, but for me it was the beginning of a liberation. I could finally read the Scriptures without having to gain immediate closure.

Can you give an example of the kinds of passages you're talking about?

Well, in the fundamentalist camp there is a sort of closet acknowledgment that there are conflicts and contradictions between the books. Proverbs is a perfect example. It's actually written along the lines of secular wisdom literature in that it says, Do this and you'll get this. Do this and this will happen to you. It recognizes cause and effect: if you live a certain way, then you'll reap the rewards or losses accordingly.

Then in Job you get this diatribe against cause and effect. Job did everything right, but he didn't get the kind of treatment you'd expect him to get if you read Proverbs. When you look at the two books side by side, there is no way to harmonize them if you're trying to build a scientific, systematic theology. They say different things.

In the fundy church we would try to explain it away by saying that Job's sin was that he didn't trust God completely. But then again neither do most of us, yet we don't lose our whole families, go bankrupt and break out in boils. It's very problematic, especially if you're trying to box it all up into a neat package. You can't do it if you're honest.

In fundamentalism we promote the Scriptures we're comfortable with and use them exhaustively. The other Scriptures we ignore or explain away. I started to realize that we would take certain texts, like the nativity and the passion narratives, and try to derive sophisticated theological truths from them. But those truths were full of holes, and I began to see those holes, even though we were determined not to see them.

For instance, the fundamentalist view of the passion is that Christ had to die for our sins to accomplish our salvation. So the whole passion narrative just leads up to that one point like a train running down a preordained track. I wondered: if that was true, then why didn't he just come down to earth and get it over with? Why all the drama if it could have ended only one way and if he knew how it would end anyway?

If you really read the passion narratives, they are about Christ antagonizing the powers that be. He ticked people off and challenged their authority. It's a much more human and social dynamic than just marching on to a predetermined conclusion. All that interaction between Jesus and the various people wasn't just to make a theological point.

The message I got was the Sadducees and Pharisees were bad and Jesus and the apostles were good. When you really read the Bible, though, it says that Jesus died at the hands of *our* sins. *We* are the people who would have crucified him, not just two sects of Judaism. We *do* crucify him every day.

But you miss all that when you reduce the passion to a theological formula that says there *had* to be a price. When you reduce it to an inevitable chain of events, you get to blame the crucifixion on "them." That's not the point. The tendency to take cosmic principles and make them into cut-and-dried theological points takes away the dynamic. It takes us out of the picture, reduces us to observers when we are really players.

The fundamentalists of the 1920s opposed science for engineering hypotheses and then trying to prove them. But fundamentalist theology does that too. It says, "Here's our hypothesis, here's our conclusion; now let's fill in the middle." That's really what some of the creation science groups are doing. The fundamentalists were right about modern science being laced with hidden agendas, but then they go and do the same thing with their theology.

As I learned to read the Scriptures without trying to prove doctrines I had already learned, I finally got to have the "aha!" experience: "Aha! It's not about me fitting reality into boxes that are manageable, it's about a lifelong, continuing discovery of God, who is too big for any box."

God doesn't change. We learned that over and over—and I'm not completely sure about it now. Well . . . that's not it exactly either. I guess what happens is that we say, "Okay, I've got this much figured out. Now—oops! I just learned something new, which changes what I thought. But God doesn't change, so I can't believe what I just learned."

It's not that God has changed, it's that I had it wrong. But when you're fighting to establish a system of boxes, you can't learn anything new. You have to put all your energy into proving the presupposed conclusions.

Choice and responsibility are denied when you think that way. You can't entertain the notion that others might be different from yourself. If they are different, they have to be wrong.

When I was developing my initial theological stances as a teenager, I couldn't understand why God wasn't responsible for sin. My logic was as follows: God is good. He gives us free will, supposedly so that we can choose to love him, but if you take the exclusivist position of fundamentalism, almost everyone who ever lived is going to burn in hell. That seems to contradict God's goodness, or at least his wisdom. Why couldn't he have made it so that almost everyone goes to heaven and only few selected bad types go to hell?

I'm not a universalist (I don't think so, anyway), but I was very impressed when Desmond Tutu spoke to our parish in South Africa. He focused on how good and loving God is. From that basis, he explained that God is going to find a way to redeem and restore everyone. That makes as much sense as the fundamentalist position that seems to have God creating people and then making damnation the most probable course of events.

Do you think that Tutu, whose compatriots were introduced to Christ by an ethnocentric colonial power, might be more inclined to see things that way than, say, a white American who has been saturated in the gospel message all his life?

I'm sure that has something to do with it. It would be a lot harder as a black South African to glibly consign victims of apartheid to damnation while affirming that their white oppressors would all sit in heaven because they got the words right.

What were you doing in South Africa, anyway?

My wife and I spent a year in a justice and reconciliation ministry. That was part of my conversion *(he laughs)* from a fundamentalist perspective of ministry. I had a strong reaction against anything that smacked of social gospel. I was taught that evangelism is ministry. Anything else might be okay to do, but it's not ministry.

So how did you backslide into the snares of the social gospel and end up wasting your time on justice and reconciliation in South Africa?

He laughs. My wife had been there several times, and she almost made it a prenuptial agreement that we would go together. I said, "I can't make it part of my vows, but I want to go." It's funny, but even though I rejected the notion that only evangelism was true ministry, I was troubled by a feeling that for much of Christendom maybe that was so.

One thing I did, just to clarify things in my own mind, was write to my previous church home and ask for financial support. I knew what the answer would be, but I wanted to do it anyway. I was somewhat of a golden boy in my church while growing up, and the scoop was that I had gone soft. I was in a "liberal" church. I had gone off to a college that they considered soft because it encouraged critical thinking about spiritual issues.

The ministry in South Africa involved helping to bring black and white Christians together to become more fully the church. This was before the dismantling of apartheid and the free elections.

I was surprised and pleased by my parents' response. They saw it as something that my wife and I wanted to do, though not truly a "mission" endeavor—but they supported us.

The church balked, as I knew it would. The head of the mission support committee had been my prayer partner when I was in high school, so we knew one another quite well. He had been something of a mentor to me for several years. He mailed me a two-page letter outlining the church's commitment to evangelistic and church-planting missions. While he felt that reconciliation was "a good thing to do," it wasn't the sort of thing the church could support as a mission activity. He went on to say that I could give the pastor a call if I wanted to discuss it further.

Did you call the pastor?

No. I knew what he would say. It's not that the church was obligated to support me. I just needed to go through the process to clarify in my own head what our growing differences were. I had been very involved there as a kid, and now I was out of the camp. That hurt, even though

I understood why it was happening. You can have a relationship with a fundamentalist, but the friendship is always overshadowed when doctrine comes up. You have probably talked to other people who have experienced this.

How did your wife respond to your church's lack of support? Was she raised in the same church?

Again, he laughs. No. She was very marginally associated with a Congregational church as a kid, so she doesn't understand my fundy issues very well. She came to Christ through a high-school campus ministry which actually has some affinities with fundamentalist thinking. She was heavily involved in a big youth camp they have in Canada. But she was never in a fundy church with all its intrigues and intertwined relationships. She can't fully identify with my knee-jerk reactions.

Can you give an example of a knee-jerk reaction?

Well, the idea that maybe I've gone soft or "liberal" still bugs me, even though I know it shouldn't. It's just part of me. We were always given that passage in Revelation about the lukewarm church and Christ wishing it was either hot or cold. There's that fear of losing the evangelistic fervor—which does happen when there's no longer a gun to your head. I always thought to myself, *If I don't go out and witness, God might hate me.* It was like *God* was holding the gun to your head . . . or the torch to your rear end.

When you're young, maybe until high school, that's not all bad. Developmentally, you do need boxes to some extent—or at least you want them so you can have closure. You also want something to kick against.

When I went to college I found a more intellectual and academic atmosphere. There was a more critical approach to the faith, although my alma mater is a very conservative evangelical school. I don't think most people would associate it with liberalism.

I think that's a safe assumption.

That college is going through one of its pendulum shifts right now, though. They are always living in the tension between the need to affirm the inerrancy of Scripture and the desire to provide a learning environment where students can ask the tough questions. Experience has shown the disadvantages of swinging too far to either extreme. If you don't teach students to think for themselves, they just become ideologues who can only speak to captive audiences. If you get too far from inerrancy, there's the chance that the Christian faith will become just one of many competing ideas with no more validity than any other belief system. Right now they're leaning more toward the inerrancy side.

I read recently in Christianity Today *that your alma mater's gay and lesbian alumni association just announced its existence, as did similar associations from other conservative Christian colleges. Could that have anything to do with the college's desire to take a more fundamentalist public stance?*

I am sure that has something to do with it. Once you speak openly about doubts and . . . aberrations, you run the risk of pulling the lids off all the little boxes. Support for the school, including both endorsements and finances, starts to dry up. But if you don't speak openly, then you have to live with the fact that you aren't looking at life as it exists.

The gay and lesbian issue is a good example. The most acceptable thing to say is that homosexual people chose to be gay—they made a choice to do something evil. But the fact is that there are people in our churches who are gay, or who at least have homosexual feelings. That situation doesn't cease to exist if we wish it away or deny it. So you learn that to stay in the church, you have to forgo owning reality.

People leave church all the time and begin owning reality outside of the church. I think that especially in fundamentalist churches there is a sense that you can't say, "Wait, I'm not experiencing this the way you are." You are expected to learn to act the way everybody says you should. You're supposed to deny what you think and feel and pretend that you think and feel something else. The trouble is that you don't get to take to Christ the reality that you feel.

As a kid I longed for a pastor who could say, "I'm struggling with my belief. I just don't believe it this week." But the pastor always acted as though his whole faith and life experience was just as it should be at all times. The congregation did the same.

In the introduction to Keith Miller's book *The Becomers,* there is a scene where an adult Sunday-school class is sitting in a circle. They go around and tell one another how God is blessing them and how everything is just fine. Then one week a new woman, who hasn't been socialized into the ways of that group, says something like, "Wow! I want to learn what you all have learned. Here's what's wrong with my life . . ."

After a long silence the woman next to her says, "Well, I haven't been totally honest," and she goes on to relate what's really going on in her life. Then another person does the same thing, and another. It's a beautiful image of a wall being let down because people discover that they are in a forgiving community where they can learn.

There is something about fundamentalist culture that forces us to say things about our lives that aren't really true and to avoid discussing the things that are really important in our lives.

Fundamentalism grew out of an unpredictable world. In the middle of war, social upheaval and the emergence of new political and religious systems, people wanted something predictable. That's understandable, but the world will always be threatening and unclear.

We all need predictability—some kind of a baseline to refer to—but to sit on it and say that we are always going to need it is dysfunctional. It is a form of arrested development.

The biggest cost for me was condemning everyone else. It was like I had saved myself, but in doing so I had separated myself from everyone else in the human race.

As you get older you see the humanity of others, and of other communities. Jesus did. He is our prime example of someone who knew who he was and what he was about, yet he didn't allow his sense of right and wrong to stand between himself and others. That has to be important. We need to know what is right and wrong, but if our sense of right and wrong closes us off from everyone else, something is not right.

2

Colorful Vegetables & the Secret Food Bank

She's a lawyer in her thirties who handles landlord-tenant disputes, AIDS-rights cases and other "do-good causes" (her term). She's active in an evangelical church within a mainline denomination that she and her parents would have formerly condemned as liberal.

Although she is a very gentle, vulnerable woman, it soon becomes evident that she is also highly intelligent. Her manner of speaking is frank and probing.

She's dressed casually. I would not have marked her as a lawyer by looking at her, but it's not hard to believe once I have spoken with her. She sits on a couch with her knees drawn up against her chest, nursing a cup of tea and a winter cold.

* * *

There was a lot of role-playing in our church—or, I should say, churches. We moved a lot because of my father's work, and we would always find a church in our denomination. I became aware quite early that my mother and father were both playing roles.

One church was in a community with a lot of migrant fruit pickers. Often, especially in the winter, poor people would stop by the church to ask for help with food and blankets. It was very cold there, so eating and staying warm were their main concerns. It troubled me when the elders would say to them, "What can we do? Let's step outside and talk."

That was their way to usher the people out of the church building so that they could send them on their way. I used to sneak out of church to see what was going on because it was so intriguing to me. Our church was all white, and most of the poor people who came by were Hispanics. They looked different—and interesting. The elders would tell them to go to the mission. They would say, "We don't have anything for you here."

The church women were supposed to be submissive to the men's authority, and that is where some of the role-playing was pretty obvious. After the elders had gone back inside my mother or one of the other ladies would flag the migrants down and take them around to the kitchen in the back of the church, where she would give them whatever we had available.

Once my mother was actually arguing with my father after he had sent someone away empty-handed. I must have been twelve or so, and I was standing there watching them quarrel. Mom nudged me, which I interpreted as a signal to chase the guy down and bring him into the kitchen, where I made small talk with him until she came back to give him some food.

You see, my mother came from a very poor family of migrant fruit pickers herself, so she knew what it's like to be poor and hungry. She understood the shame and loneliness of poverty in a way that my father didn't. My father and most of the other men saw poverty as a moral stigma. It was as though destitution was an outward sign of moral failure on the poor person's part. My mother knew better from her own experience.

That image of the elders turning cold and hungry people away from the front door of the church and the women sneaking them around back for some food is still very vivid in my mind. It was one of my most formative impressions of church life from my childhood years.

Sometimes my mother would deliberately buy groceries to keep in the church cupboard. There was no concept of a food bank back then (or at least not in our church), but Mom and a few other women had an informal food cupboard. They also kept firewood on hand for people who had no heat. And they were always rounding up blankets.

This was all done on the sly. Outwardly the women were the model of submissive Christian womanhood, deferring to the men in authority. But they knew that Christ would have helped, so they had to help.

By the time I was thirteen or so, I wanted to organize the food cupboard openly. I took some of my allowance and began to stock the cupboard. Mom said, "Yeah . . . well . . . maybe." She couldn't come right out and say it was a good idea, because she and Dad fought about it a lot. But she had to drive me to the store, since I was too young to drive, so she got drawn into my scheme. She suggested that maybe we could hide the stuff in the trunks of cars.

Soon Mom and I, and a few others, were stockpiling nonperishable foods, blankets and whatever else we could find. People came and got the help they needed. Some of them stuck around to talk, and we followed up with a few of them. One family even joined the church eventually.

My food cupboard was tolerated because I was the church's problem child and they wanted to see me straighten out. (I was the recipient of many prayers.) They had some heated discussions at the elders' meeting—the usual white Republican sentiments about the poor—but ultimately they let me stock the food cupboard because they saw it as a "sort of positive" sign that my rebelliousness was being channeled in a good direction.

I would have done it anyway. What were they going to say—"you can't use that empty space"? I think that's what they wanted to say, but they had consciences, even if they didn't always act on them the way I thought they should have.

You say that you were perceived as a problem child. Were you into drugs and liquor and that sort of thing?

Oh no! Not at all. No drugs. No sex. No rock 'n' roll. I just asked too many questions. I was actually what many people would call a good girl. But I just didn't have that natural awe of people in authority. At least not if I thought they were being hypocritical.

I always spoke up. Elders took me aside many times and told me that I had a very bad attitude. I was not at all sweet about it. I was *very* angry. At that time my father was an elder, and he was quite abusive in our home. Everything had to look perfect. It made me sensitive to the hypocrisy in the church.

The elders did try to minister to me in their own way. I have to give them that. They had a lawyer in the congregation teach a Sunday-school class on antinomies of faith. Those are teachings that seem to contradict other teachings. I'm sure that came about partly because of me. I would hear about God blessing us in war and ask, "What about 'Thou shalt not kill'?" I wasn't trying to be troublesome, I just wanted to reconcile what I saw to be contradictory—like the conflict between Jesus' teachings about the poor and the deacons' sending hungry people away in the winter cold.

It was meaningful for me that someone cared enough to try to address my big questions. We even got to the point where we did acknowledge that, at least superficially, there were some apparent contradictions in the Bible.

My mother really helped me to bridge the gap between following Christ and following the peculiarities of our church. She was the first woman to wear pants to church. Oh yes! She wore a pantsuit, and that was pretty exciting. She couldn't see any reason not to, so she did.

She was the Sunday-school superintendent, and she started busing kids to Sunday school. She'd go around the neighborhood telling people that our bus would pick their kids up and bring them back. Surprisingly, most parents saw that as a good deal, even if they didn't come to church themselves.

That was another problem for our church elders. They generally liked the idea of evangelizing, but the kids my mother was bringing were mostly Hispanic. They were particularly negative about having non-English-speaking kids in Sunday school. It wasn't a problem for my mother.

There were lots of bilingual kids who translated. To me the elders' response seemed racist and hypocritical. It caused me a lot of hurt.

Mom got lots of criticism over the busing. The easiest thing would have been to drop it and just get back inside the fortress and pull up the drawbridge. But here's the surprise: my father drove the bus! He was very clear on evangelism and saw that as a whole different issue from giving out food and blankets. If it was going to evangelize someone, he would do it. If he hadn't supported Mom in that way, she would have had to cave in.

The role of women was a real stumbling block for me, and if my mother had not shown me that she didn't buy the whole submission thing either, I might have had a bigger crisis of faith than I did.

Once the preacher's sermon was on the need for women to serve colorful vegetables to their husbands. *She laughs.* I'm not kidding! I remember it almost verbatim. He said that a woman should serve her husband at least two colors of vegetables with dinner. I thought that it had to be a joke. I came to church to hear the Word of God, and here was this guy going off about colorful vegetables! I would have just left the building in tears, but my mother nudged me and whispered, "I'll bet he's had a fight with his wife over this."

That helped. But people just sat there taking it all in as though it was the gospel. Why didn't someone stop him?

They had big arguments about women teaching Sunday school. It was okay for them to teach children, but was it right for a woman to teach men in a class? Apparently not.

Dad and Mom wanted good adult education, and they both thought that if someone was really qualified, it was wrong not to use their talents. But there was a lot of resistance.

I remember our time in that church as a daily battle. We were "active" church members, which meant that we were in church at least three times a week, often five times. In my mind I remember each of those times as a big struggle over issues like my mother's pantsuit, colorful vegetables and giving blankets to cold people. It was very difficult.

After I left for college my mother had a reaction. She just stopped going to church altogether. I'm not sure what precipitated that decision, but for years now she hasn't been a member anywhere. She recently started going to a more accepting church (one that we would have called liberal), but she only goes infrequently.

My father fought her for ten years, but not too long ago he dropped his membership and told Mom, "I will go with you wherever you go."

That must have been a huge jump for your father.

I really respect his love for my mother in doing that. We used to have to find a church in our denomination every time we moved. It was an article of faith. Dad would have denounced the church he goes to now as apostate. It's actually a very orthodox, vibrant Christian community.

My father was not as hardheaded as many of the other elders, though. He did take us to movies, even if they were just Disney movies. That was nearly a scandal.

Some fundamentalists back then would not even go to Billy Graham movies because they were shown in the same theaters as Hollywood movies. That may have been the reason that we set up a screen and projector in the church to see Billy Graham movies. Movies were a huge no-no.

Dad supported Mom in her career. We would hear lots of oblique statements like "We have a family in this congregation where the woman works outside the home!" That was another huge no-no.

When did you actually leave home?

I deliberately went off to a state university in another city to get away from that stifling church situation. I just had to go. My father did everything but tie me to a chair to keep me from going. Boy, did we have some fights!

I went to college to major in philosophy, to see if Christianity could hold its own against other ideas and belief systems. I wanted to follow Jesus, but I didn't want to hold to someone else's *idea* of Jesus.

At first I was so depressed about what church was, as opposed to what it could be, that to go to a church would have brought me to tears. But an interesting thing happened. I had to wait two days for a dorm room, since they were very scarce. I finally got a place in a cluster suite where all the girls were Christians. They listened to me and told me that there were lots of churches near the university. They even took me and showed me where they were.

They all went to a small church that met in a little movie theater. I asked them about it, and they said I might not feel comfortable there but they would love for me to come.

I went, and it sure was different from my home church! The preacher was a young bearded guy in overalls. There was a woman in overalls who played the fiddle, and that was the music. We all sang along.

It was the first time I had ever been to a charismatic church, and it was pretty traumatic for me. They would raise their hands and sing in the Spirit, but they weren't foaming at the mouth or anything, and I felt the love of people who were living a Christian life. That church was a real gift.

The church was very active in college life. A lot of the members were former fundamentalists. Soon we grew out of the movie house. Eventually the church got big and joined a denomination.

If you had to put it in a few words, what was the most profound difference between that church and your home church?

They weren't in the fortress mentality. If it's fun and not a sin—do it! We were out in the world, but not of the world. We could have a beer, go to a movie and listen to music. The faith wasn't about *not* doing things. It was about action. That church had a positive impact on many, many college students like me. I was pretty timid about some things, so I wasn't the one who was pushing. I didn't drink a beer for years, and when I finally did I didn't like it anyway. But it was great to feel like there were other people thinking about things. That church was exciting and vigorous. It was primarily a church of young people.

Their perspective was that there were enough real sins in the world—such as sexual immorality, greed, cruelty and so forth—that we didn't need to invent our own list. If it wasn't a stumbling block, it was probably okay. That freed me up to think about real questions. I didn't have to worry about pants and colorful vegetables anymore. I could think about justice and righteousness. It was okay to think about hunger and homelessness.

I was very excited, and I tried unsuccessfully to get my parents to visit the church. My father refused. He said that it was nothing but a hothouse church for a bunch of overintelligent people.

After three years my parents did come. They came quite a few times, in fact, and they finally were able to acknowledge that it was a valid, God-worshiping body of believers.

My mother is a very intelligent woman. She always had a crosscultural sensitivity from her experience with poverty as a child. My father can't understand on such a deep level, but his mind isn't entirely closed. I'm glad that my parents were willing to make themselves uncomfortable for me. I've always been able to make *them* uncomfortable.

So they weren't as close-minded as many of the other people in that church, and that's partly why I stayed in the faith. If some of those other people had been my parents, I don't know how it would have turned out.

How does your fundamentalist upbringing affect you today?

It still makes it hard for me to live in grace. I often slip into a performance mode: Am I doing enough? Am I winning enough souls? I still feel that I exist to do good works for God, and that really gets me down.

I think if there had been a Protestant order of nuns who had a structured regimen, I might have said, "Okay, I'll do what you say." I spent so long on my knees praying for a mission, as in a mission field. I think that I wanted to be off the hook, to have it all taken out of my hands. But God says, "No, you have to live with the rest of them."

On the positive side, I suppose that my experience is the reason why, as a lawyer, I gravitate toward cases involving needy people. I want to do good. And I love it. The people who really need a lawyer can't afford one.

My husband and I are going through a divorce right now. Along with the pain of separation is that old sense of guilt and failure. We'll both continue to worship at this church, so there is also that whole issue of how it must look to others.

It is still hard to trust elders, pastors and other male authorities in the church. For a young woman, the intimidation of facing all those men who are so sure of their own anointing is so painful that I can't describe it. Racial discrimination must be like that—facing people who are mistreating you, crushing your spirit and so arrogant they don't even know it.

My positive church experience was with the women. They were the ones who had the walk and walked the talk. Being under more female leadership, as more women take authority positions in the church, is very therapeutic for me. After so long, it's hard to trust the guys anymore.

I have known people who completely left the faith. They were as miserable as I was, and when they got loose they just kept running. I think that part of the reason I'm still a Christian is that I fought back. I didn't just sit on the pain and anger until I had to walk away.

If you had to explain fundamentalism to someone, how would you begin?

Fundamentalists have to have something to put on the other side of the fence. It might be going to movies, gambling, dancing, abortion or whatever. The fence is the thing. It separates Us from Them.

Anthropological studies of fundamentalist movements in other cultures show a similar pattern. We don't get into that fundamentalist mindset just because we're Christians. We get into it out of fear and a need for sure answers.

The whole phenomenon of people who dropped out of the faith in their teens and twenties, yet are returning in their thirties and forties, is both positive and negative for me. Those who are just looking for an escape from the mess we have made of the world could become like the fundamentalists of my childhood. We all could fall into that trap as we get older and want more security and less chaos.

It will take some spiritual insight. The specific issues will be different, but the motivation could be very similar. We all have a need to be right, and if the new generation just comes up with their own list of rights and wrongs, we will not have made any progress. Being right isn't the same thing as submitting to Christ.

3

Their Theology Wasn't Bad, Just Immature

Jacob is a fortysomething artist and college professor who maintains strong ties with former students even after they have embarked on their own careers. His home is filled with his own paintings, those of former students and a small but elegant collection of modern masters. He has had several long-term, live-in relationships, but his avant-garde lifestyle and penchant for traveling have conspired to keep him unmarried.

Marie is his sister, younger by a year, a business professional. As children they were particularly close, attending church, youth group and summer camp together. In high school some assumed they were boyfriend and girlfriend. Marie attended a fundamentalist college in the Midwest after high school. Jacob went off to a big state university in another city.

Sitting with them is Chuck, Marie's husband of twenty years. Chuck and Jacob became friends through school activities, but Chuck did not know Marie well until they shared a summer job.

Chuck and Marie are active in an evangelical church. Jacob became estranged from his childhood church during the Vietnam War and never formally returned. It was Jacob who suggested a joint, brother-sister interview. Chuck asked to sit in as an observer.

* * *

JACOB: We were really close throughout our childhood. Not like boyfriend and girlfriend, though. Maybe like twins. We lived away from town, and we spent a lot of time working with our parents in the family store. Church was our social life.

MARIE: I don't remember as much as he does. For me childhood was a blur—not looking forward or backward or to the side. It was like I grew up with tunnel vision.

JACOB: I admired Marie because she was always at task. I couldn't live as disciplined a life as she did. She always finished her piano lessons while I just muddled through. She always got better grades. I just figured that she was smarter than me. Back then I saw no distinction between grades and intelligence.

College was where I began to see a whole new world of possibilities. At college they weren't just looking at grades, at least not back in the sixties when I was there. I wanted to go to a school where I could think freely. We had attended a Christian high school that I found very constricting. I got in trouble for reading comic books and listening to music. One teacher kept telling us that our parents were sinning because they worked on Sunday, even though they were moonlighting as janitors for a church. My folks took that job when the family store couldn't support the Christian school tuition.

But I never really questioned too much as a kid. I went to church and listened to the sermons just like everyone else. That was church. *He turns to Marie.* I couldn't just believe it all like you did.

MARIE: I didn't believe it at all! I always felt guilty that I *didn't* believe it. That's why I went to a Christian college—I wanted to test my faith. If it didn't work, I was going to dump it.

JACOB: Really? *He seems truly surprised.* I just knew that I didn't want to have a lot of questions yet go to a school that allowed no questions. After you went to college I felt like I couldn't talk to you freely anymore, and—

MARIE: *(Cutting him off)* I remember coming home and you thinking I was a square. It was like I was a project. You would take me to movies and dances and have me listen to new music. It was like you thought I had been on another planet.

JACOB: If you felt that way, why didn't you say something?

MARIE: I just told you. Life was like a tunnel for me. I didn't feel that I had any right to say or do anything. At church the preacher talked. After the movies you would talk. I just listened.

JACOB: Well, why didn't you say what you thought about things?

MARIE: That wasn't my place. When we were kids, you would lead and I would follow. I didn't mind it. I didn't feel controlled by you. That was just the way it was. My life was like that.

After a long pause, she continues. I shut down emotionally after that time I was sexually assaulted. I know you didn't know about it—nobody did until much later. It drove me into a holding pattern. I just didn't feel things. That was why I went to a Christian college. I wanted to see if this faith I was supposed to have was real or if it was just something imposed on me.

JACOB: I'll have to think about that. I thought you were the one with the strong faith. I thought you really believed.

MARIE: Well, you were wrong.

JACOB: Hmm. I'm finding this all pretty surprising. See, I have felt closer to you because in talking to Chuck I have seen that he's not stuck in the fundamentalist mode. That has made me think that maybe you have come along some too.

MARIE: You mean that you're surprised that I'm not the same Christian that I was in 1964? Nobody is. You're not. I'm not. Look at how the non-Christian world has changed. When we were in a Christian school, the public schools wouldn't let girls wear pants or take shop or even get into the top science classes. You have a problem with your *image* of me more than with me.

CHUCK: If I could interject here . . . *He looks at me. I shrug. Then he addresses Jacob.* Marie has led *me,* not the other way around. When I got out of the army I was pretty screwed up, as you probably remember. I went from Joe Christian to Joe Hippie, then back to Joe Fundamentalist. Marie is the one who has led the real probing discussions.

At this point we go off the record as the three of them get close to some painful family history, including Marie's sexual abuse by a close family friend. After a long discussion Chuck and Marie feel it best that they leave so I can interview Jacob alone.

That was surprising. Marie and I love one another very much, but we have been emotionally estranged for a long time. I guess we both assumed a lot about each other.

For me being a Christian was not an issue. It was like being an American. You just *were* one, so you tried to be a good one. You couldn't choose not to be one. I was born and raised in the faith, and even now, though I don't go to church at all, it's hard to talk without putting things in Christian terms.

I remember accepting Christ when I was nine or ten, and it was a very poignant thing, but it was also just part of life. Same with my baptism later on. I never had doubts. Just questions. When I asked questions that the church people didn't want to deal with, I never doubted that there were answers. I think they saw my asking as a lack of faith, but at that point the freedom to ask was built on faith that there were answers.

I had tried to understand doctrine, and when it didn't make sense I would ask my Sunday-school teachers, "Why? What is the reason? How do you *know?*" They spoke with certainty, but they wouldn't give me any answers. That was a clue.

Whenever they didn't want to answer they would just tell me to have faith. That was when I realized that I had a different way of thinking about religion. They almost took pride in not questioning, as if it made them more spiritual.

History made me question, though. The Nazis took power because not enough people questioned. We learned that in school. Those Germans were scorned for not questioning. But then when I questioned the Vietnam War, it made me a suspect and cast doubt on me—like maybe I was a godless commie.

In junior high we would see these Red Scare movies where the communists take over the world. Those movies seemed very real, and they seemed to be saying that we should be vigilant. That made sense to me. But what impressed me most was that church people used logic when it suited them, and when it didn't they would say, "Have faith."

It all came to a head for me during the Vietnam War. I was in college, so I was exposed to lots of new ways of looking at life. In church we had the U.S. flag right up front with the cross and the Bible. On the wall we would have the soldier of the week.

I felt early on that the war was wrong, so my stance became a big issue in the church. It was easy for me to point out the poor logic that people used in support of the war, and it was just as easy for them to fall back on the "have faith" response. The big issue was that I was questioning, which they saw as doubting.

I wasn't asked to leave the church, but the deacons and ministerial staff saw me as controversial and kept me on a tight leash. I had been the president of the youth group, but now I was doubting the wisdom of men who had supposedly been told what was right by God.

History has proven them wrong on Vietnam. From the pulpit we would hear about God being on our side and how the United States was God's instrument for fighting the yellow heathens. But it wasn't true. Now it's the same with issues like abortion. Those same people use the same logic: "God told me."

Their logic led them into a corner. When God is on your side, what you think is what God thinks. You can do anything. The trouble is that every army has a god. The winner has *the* God. Luckily those people were born in America. If they had been born in Saudi Arabia they would be the heathens.

Finally there were just too many things that you couldn't bring up in church. Now it's not Vietnam, it's gays. And people have the same confident, God-told-me attitude. The best research seems to suggest that being gay is more genetic than moral or religious, but that is not what they want to hear. It can't be a chemical difference in the brain. It has to be that gays are terrible sinners.

Young people in every era will have big questions that need answers, or at least a serious hearing. But at church the answer is just "Have faith." So they keep losing the people who ask questions.

I wanted to know how we could be so sure that people like us were going to heaven while everybody else went to hell. Boy, did I question! My church was white, and it didn't really want any blacks. I asked if there would be two heavens: one white, one black. I started to look for an inclusive Christianity because I couldn't imagine a loving God saving my church and sending everybody in Africa to hell.

I had trouble with the church picking out one or two sins that were especially bad, when their own doctrine said that *all* have fallen short of the glory of God. It seemed like they just wanted to enforce their own likes and dislikes. I finally came to the understanding that there is one God who has a lot of different names.

My church claimed to be literal interpreters of the Bible. They could say with certainty, This is a sin, this isn't. Therefore women had to wear hats. That was a biblical truth. But if Scripture is infallible, one of those truths is that the earth is the center of creation. They would fudge on that one, but not on the hats.

Catholics, whom they did not consider Christian, took a literal approach to Communion: it became the actual flesh and blood of Christ. They would chuckle at that.

Fundamentalism is like the Santa Claus theory. You believe it when you're a kid, but everyone hopes that you don't grow up believing it. When fundamentalism has lost its purpose, it is discarded for something more profound.

I don't feel any ill will for the simplistic truths I was taught as a child. The theology wasn't bad, just immature. Evangelicalism and fundamentalism are trying to keep everyone believing in Santa. I have just come to accept additional ideas that are outside of Christianity.

4

Does *Anyone* Stay in Fundamentalism?

She's a gracious, talkative and disarmingly open woman in her late thirties. Ten years ago she was divorced from an abusive husband and was nearly bankrupt. Now she is married to a highly successful executive who seems to delight in her very being. She lives what many people would consider the American dream.

We sit at a large kitchen table looking out over a neighborhood of spacious homes. The architecture and landscaping are upscale but not ostentatious. Children ride bikes on the quiet streets. Neighbors visit in front yards and cul-de-sacs. Her landscaped back yard abuts a greenbelt where one of her sons has parked his Tonka earth-moving equipment in a big pile of dirt.

The housing development rests in a quiet valley at the end of a long, winding road. Her husband's commute into the city takes nearly an hour. She teaches in a nearby school district. Although other housing developments make the area quite populated, it feels as though we're in a small village at the edge of a dense forest. The trees, verdant with early summer foliage, rustle in a gentle breeze. A cacophony of songbirds, happy children and an ice-cream truck's musical horn fill the air.

Our interview is punctuated by visits from her children (and their friends), ranging in age from kindergarten to upper grade school, curious about why anyone would put their mother in a book. Not one of them can remember to close the screen door to keep out the wasps and yellowjackets, yet their forgetfulness only amuses her.

* * *

My folks are a prime example of what I would consider a fundamentalist mindset, particularly my mother. Don't get me wrong. I love my folks, and I get along quite well with them, but they are perfect clients for what the fundamentalists are selling.

They have also been involved in some extreme political groups. Not hate groups or anything like that, but ultraconservative groups that want someone who will blindly follow their agenda.

My mother, bless her heart, is pretty unsophisticated, and when she gets caught up in a movement or an idea, she takes on this terrific zeal and just goes for it. While someone else might think it through a bit more and say, "Oh, boy, this isn't good," she'll just charge ahead.

I hated our fundamentalist church, and I don't believe I got one positive thing from it. Does *anyone* stay in fundamentalism? It seems like everyone that I grew up with left as soon as they were old enough. Fundamentalists alienate so many people!

I remember at age eight or nine spending every Sunday morning, Sunday evening and Wednesday evening thinking about three things as I sat in that pew: Jonathan, a boy I had a crush on; *boy, are my legs skinny* (I spent a lot of time looking down); and *I hate these people.* They were so negative and exclusive. Everyone outside the fundamentalist circle was doomed to hell.

Do you remember those double-knit suits that were in fashion in the seventies? Well, our pastor wore a red one. Even as a little kid I remember watching him in that horrible suit, leaning over the pulpit, condemning everyone to hell. I thought, *You can't even dress yourself. I'm not listening to you!*

Weren't there any positive ideas or themes you got at all?

None. The people were just too mean and narrow. They put down everyone who was different from them, and they gossiped about one another right there in the church: "Oh, look what so-and-so is wearing! Did you hear what such-and-such's kid did?" It never stopped.

Did you talk to your parents about your unhappiness with the church?

Not really. I wanted to be a good girl and please my folks, so I did what was expected of me. My brothers were a different story. They got jobs at gas stations and stores and then lined up Sunday and Wednesday shifts so they wouldn't have to go to church.

My mother, as I said, is not a sophisticated person. She trudged off to church week after week because she thought it was the right thing to do. My father was a bit of a mystery. His job was quite demanding, and it was in a government agency so he couldn't talk about it. I really didn't know what he did for a living. We didn't talk much.

The high point of my high-school graduation ceremony was when I got the first positive comment I ever remember from Dad. He said, "We're proud of you." I was bowled over.

We're close now, but back then he was just wrapped up in his work. That's what fathers did in those days. Now I really like him as a person. He's interested in my kids, and I'm interested in fishing and some other things that he likes to do.

But back then I just suffered along in silence. It got worse and worse as the years went on, so that I just couldn't stand it. The idea of going to church almost made me physically sick, but off I went to please my folks.

I do remember my mother and I talking about it once, now that I think of it. She went to see the pastor for counseling over one of my brothers, who was getting into some fairly serious trouble with drugs. The pastor just laughed at her and said, "Your son is a total loss as a human being." He dismissed her with that statement.

He literally laughed at her?

Yes. Right in her face. She was terribly upset, and I asked her outright, "Mom, why did you go to *him* for advice? He's a bozo!" Her response surprised me, because she didn't really contradict me. She said in a resigned sort of way, "Well, yes, but he *is* the pastor."

How long did you keep going to that church with your parents?

Until I was twenty and in college. I finally decided to tell my folks that I just couldn't do it anymore, so I gave them a week to get used to the idea. I told my mother that I loved and respected them and didn't want to hurt their feelings, but that for my own sanity and self-respect, I couldn't go to that church anymore. Mom always listened to me, so she said that was okay. I wasn't sure what my father would think.

That Sunday I hauled myself out of bed thinking how great it would be to stay away from that awful church. I could read the paper, have a cup of coffee. But I found my folks sitting around in their bathrobes. I said, "Mom, Dad, you'll be late for church!" They looked a bit sheepish and said, "Well, honey, we didn't like it much either, so we're going to sit it out for a while."

I couldn't believe it! I almost . . . I *did* scream, "You mean I didn't have to go all this time?" My folks never went back again. After a few weeks a woman my mother knew from the church came by and asked where they had been. She wondered if they had been ill. Mom just told her that they were reexamining their thinking. She was still undecided at that point. But not for long.

What cemented it was the way those people treated them. In stores they would look the other way and pretend Mom and Dad weren't there. They gossiped about them and called them backsliders. They complained that Mom and Dad weren't tithing—which is supposed to be a secret anyway.

After all those years when I went to church three times a week, sang in the choir and went to youth group, that's how it ended. I used to work in the nursery, taking care of their babies (although that was partly to avoid sitting in church). There wasn't a kind word. Nobody asked me how I was doing or said they missed me. It just ended one Sunday.

You said that the pastor in the red suit was a very negative influence. Didn't you have a youth pastor you could connect with?

Youth pastors came and went pretty quickly. The only message I got was, You're worthless until you accept Christ, and then you're *still* pretty worthless.

I always felt that I was special. I think everyone does. But I just kept getting hammered with how worthless I was. How dismal!

Did you accept Christ while you were in that church?

Oh yes. I was baptized by immersion and the whole thing. At the time it was real to me because I wanted to do what was right. My father always told us not to mess up the family name, and I took that to mean that I should try to be a good Christian. I thought being a Christian meant that I had to try to accept their views. I worked hard in school, read a lot and didn't get in trouble with boys. Well, I remember sneaking out with a boy once, but we didn't go rolling around or anything.

I should say that I believed the religious ideas that I was being taught, but not the way those ideas were manifested in the lives of the people at church. They weren't kindhearted, which is big in my book; they weren't funny, which is also big in my book. They were just mean and petty, which negated everything they taught.

I learned that what you say and what you do are different, and so I learned to live two lives. There was the real me and the me that sat in the church pew week after week, listening obediently to all that drivel that I totally rejected. Yet I was probably, in their eyes, a pretty good kid.

I wanted to be a good kid, but I wanted to have some integrity in my own life, some personal space. I learned pretty early that you can get anything if you're quiet. I would spend time in my room reading, and I had a good experience in my Christian school, so I could be two people. I was the good girl who stayed out of trouble, and I was also the girl who thought the whole show was a big farce.

I saw other kids rebel, and it seemed to just get them more grief. It was self-destructive and ignorant—drinking, taking drugs, promiscuity. They seemed to suffer more from their rebellion than anyone they were rebelling against. I think that I knew enough of what I believed, or didn't believe, so that I didn't have to go crazy fighting against the system. I knew that wild rebellion was just the flip side of that unhappy, life-smothering religion.

How did the fundamentalist church experience affect you later in life?

I am still sorting that one out. My first marriage was to a very uptight man who made a career in the military. He was terribly manipulative and dishonest, a real control freak. Late in the marriage he got quite abusive, though not physically.

I sometimes wonder if my childhood ability to live two lives had something to do with that. I can't imagine why I married him! Or why I stuck with him for eight years! He lied about everything, even the most insignificant things. He loved the military, but he lied to them too. I wonder if things would have been different if I had lived one life as a child rather than two.

His military training was quite similar to the fundamentalist training I had as a kid: "Here's what you believe. Here's what you do."

I'm sure some people go through military training and keep it in perspective, but he was consumed by the training. That was his life, and it didn't do anything to improve him as a person. It just drove him into a little enclosed world with its own set of realities and values. He gave everything over to the military, and it made him a much worse person. I more or less watched it happen, hoping that he would come around. I had assumed that we thought alike, but it became more and more obvious that we didn't.

Part of the initial attraction was that he knew exactly what he wanted to be and I had never really met anyone like that, who had such a strong sense of self. The kids I grew up with were all wishy-washy, rebellious or hypocritical. I just didn't understand *what* he wanted to be until it was too late.

Did your fundamentalist training make you feel that divorce was immoral or wrong?

That didn't even enter into it. I never considered it in that way. My problem was that I just didn't realize I had the power to do what I needed to do. I didn't know that I could just make a choice and do it.

I remember one night—we had been married a couple of years—he and a friend were sitting on the couch. He was cleaning his weapon, and he said, "I have the power of life and death over regular people." I had to get up and leave. I went for a walk and called my mother. I said, "Mom, I think I've made a huge mistake." She said, "Well, honey, he *is* your husband. It will be okay." There wasn't a framework to consider that maybe I should get a divorce. So after my walk I came back and lived as his wife for several years, even though I knew it was wrong.

I stayed married to him until he got really strange and frightening and abusive, and then I got divorced. It was hard on my kids, and they have divorced him too.

You said that your Christian school experience was positive. Was it a fundamentalist school?

The school was small, and it taught pretty much the same thing that my church taught, but some of the teachers lived it very differently. We had some teachers who really loved us. They liked us personally, not for what they could make us into.

I learned a lot from them, but not so much from what they said as from how they lived. I had learned to pay scant attention to people's words. But I did learn values from those teachers, and I am like them in some ways. I like my kids, and I like it when they do kid stuff. When children do something that causes a problem, it's usually because they're interested in finding something out. They're not losers. For example, when my son was little, he used to talk about poo-poo. I said, "That's okay, but not at dinner with guests." I wanted him to learn when to do some things and when not to. But I like that process, and I like kids for being kids.

Right now one of my sons is grounded from tools. He's not a bad kid, but when he gets a saw or a hammer, he has to try it out and doesn't seem to understand which things are not suitable for sawing or nailing—like the walls and furniture. But I would never tell him that he is an evil loser. He's just a kid, and those are the kinds of things kids do.

Some of my teachers were like that when my classmates and I did childish things. Their love wasn't conditional on a set of behaviors.

They liked us *because* we were kids, not in spite of it.

I became a teacher after being fairly successful in another career, and when they asked me why I wanted to be a teacher, I said this: "Every person on this earth has a spark. It might be a skill, an aptitude or a way of relating to people. If people feel safe, they can blossom." That was what the fundamentalists couldn't do. They couldn't let us feel safe.

Would your teachers—the ones you liked so much—have considered themselves fundamentalists?

Not in the same way. Here's an example. I know there is a passage in the Bible that says that when you have a problem with someone, you go to that person rather than gossiping about them. My teachers lived that way, and then *later* they might have said that the Bible taught that. They lived it and then taught it, in contrast to my church, which taught it but didn't attempt to live it.

We did have some teachers who taught like this: "Here's the dogma. Write it down. Class is over. See you later." The other teachers believed the same things, but their care for us was louder than their dogma.

I have taken the things that I want from Christianity. My husband and I have been talking about going back to church, for the sake of our kids. But maybe we would be doing something as wrong as what was done to us. He describes himself as a recovering Catholic, and his childhood was much like mine as far as guilt and hypocrisy go. But we haven't felt enough need to get involved in a church.

We have been reading William Bennett's *The Book of Virtues,* which we both find very helpful. We believe in doing your personal best in everything. My husband models that for my children. He's very successful and well regarded in the community, but he lives it before he preaches it.

So now we try to live and teach core values, but without the religious wrapping. We celebrate Christmas, but it's a time for family togetherness. It's not about the baby Jesus. And Easter—well, that was always pretty weird for me to put together. You've got Jesus rising from the dead and a little fluffy bunny dropping candy eggs around the house. What's that supposed to teach a kid?

As a family we are very conservative. We believe in moral values, family bonding and giving back your talents to society. I don't know if *conservative* is the right word, but I think you know what I mean. I guess I see Christian teaching as a smorgasbord where you take what you like and can use, and leave the rest on the table.

5

Each Point of View Contains Its Own Duality

He's a business consultant in his late forties who grew up in a conservative church and attended one of America's most conservative fundamentalist colleges. His parting with fundamentalist Christianity was gradual, not predicated on any one issue or event.

In the seventies he was drawn to est, Werner Erhard's controversial workshops. Now married with children, he continues his association with est, which is called Landmark Educational Forum in its latest manifestation.

* * *

The smug exclusiveness of fundamentalism struck me even at a very early age. I recall being in perhaps third grade when a man in our church asked me what I believed. Then he said, "Did you know that if you died right now, you would go to hell?" I hadn't known this. Then he asked me if I would rather go to heaven. I quickly replied, "Sure!"

It was like he was asking me if I wanted a free trip to Hawaii or something. That always got to me. It was like Christianity was an insurance policy, but instead of paying premiums you had this "thing" you had to do.

But you did as he said?

Oh yes. He was an adult, so I figured that he knew what he was talking about. I was a believer all through high school, at least in certain areas, but an awareness of that fundamentalist arrogance was always in the background. It's one thing to say that you are interpreting, second- or thirdhand, what God has revealed. It's something else to say that you speak God's truth unfiltered. That's blasphemy, isn't it?

Later another man in our church sold me on the idea of going to a fundamentalist college in the South. My parents didn't really push it, but he did, and I respected him, so I just went. He's a fine guy who I still count as a friend. I have no anger about it.

Actually I enjoyed school. We had to wear jackets and ties, and you couldn't physically touch a girl. You couldn't go off campus on a date either. They had a dating parlor, which some students called "the furniture store" because it was full of couches and chairs. They also jokingly called it "the passion pit." You could go there to talk, but there was always a senior student keeping a watchful eye.

Again, that didn't bother me much. I had been raised to think that good Christians behaved that way, so it wasn't a problem. We could also take a date to services, plays and other activities on the campus. One winter evening a bunch of guys and one girl were going out, and the girl slipped on the ice and hurt herself. None of the guys offered to help her up, because you weren't supposed to touch girls. Then later *(he laughs)* a female faculty member heard about it and was furious that nobody even helped the girl! But that was how we were taught—so hey, what are you going to do?

I left that school after two years to go to another Christian school closer to home, but I don't think I had any sense of anger as I left. My second school was similar, but not nearly as restrictive. They didn't have dances or wild parties, but you could leave the campus. It was a much more normal environment.

When you stopped going to church and began your association with est, was there a particular turning point?

Not really. I became more aware as I entered high school and college that there were two points of view, according to the Christians I knew: God's, which they articulated, and all others. In science, philosophy, literature and other disciplines, each point of view had its own basis, which led to my simultaneous universe theory.

There are many points of view, and each contains its own duality. Most arguments are not conversations because they are about two separate dualities talking past one another.

Can you give an example? You're losing me here.

Look at history. There was a tribal period when people were members of a certain tribe or they were aliens. In the theistic period they were believers in the true God or they weren't. The Greeks stressed reason: people were operating rationally or irrationally. In the period of the state, people were either loyal or traitorous.

We tend to make one duality our own and act as though the others either don't exist or aren't valid. I came to understand that life is built on a continuum, and on each continuum there are people at either end and at points in between. For some the measuring stick is whether an idea is scientific or unscientific. In sports it's winning or losing.

In our age we are very influenced by entertainment. Something is either interesting or not. Business is either profitable or unprofitable. Education—I used to be a public-school teacher—has its own duality too: right or wrong. Right answers versus wrong answers. That's the reality of education.

I became increasingly convinced that all of these positions are valid, and, in fact, each position is held by someone. I could have propounded this perspective at the two Christian colleges I attended, but I would have been in hot water had I suggested that all these positions are valid, or that they are all equal.

Even though you have rejected fundamentalism, you don't seem to have the anger or frustration that some of my other subjects have with it. Do you feel that fundamentalism is an equal duality?

Certainly. It gives you access to a moral universe—a safe, knowable, friendly world. You don't have to deal with existential angst.

There is a sense of community, historical continuity and connection with the universe, with something larger than yourself.

The built-in limits are fairly clear, but it's a workable reality for many people. It preaches, more than it practices, service. Service becomes a way to get brownie points or status. But if you want to perform real service, the opportunity is there. Fundamentalism, like any other duality, creates a "because universe," a world where everything happens for a knowable reason. There's great peace in that, although fundamentalism does limit your ability to live in the present somewhat because it is so oriented to the past and future.

So you don't feel a need to do battle with those elements of fundamentalism that you disagree with, because it's a valid belief system? Even though fundamentalism would reject your belief system as wrong?

Sure. Besides, most discussions are one duality against a different duality. If two people are discussing an issue based on reason, or outcome, or profit and loss, they are operating from the same duality, and they can end up somewhere different from where they began. But if one person is saying, "This is right because God says so," and the other person objects on the basis of reason or the historical record, then each person is just delivering a monologue, and you can't discuss with someone who's delivering a monologue. Talking with that person takes time and energy, but it can't lead anywhere, so there's no reason to argue.

Are these your own ideas, or did you glean these from your est training?

Est helped facilitate my thinking, but the ideas were germinating in me from an early age. Est isn't a religion, but that is an example of how difficult it is to talk to people in another duality. Actually, people who come to est with religious beliefs usually find that their belief system becomes more profound and meaningful. But then there are some people who come to est itself with an evangelical fervor, as though it was a religion, or Amway or something.

Most people live a problem-centered life. By constantly trying to find the solution to the problem, they actually reinforce the problem.

It's like a man who has a problem with his mother. He can't get away from his mother. He takes her with him everywhere he goes because his life is centered on the problem of his mother. That may be the way some ex-fundamentalists feel about fundamentalism. They are trying to speak to one duality, fundamentalism, with a new duality like logic, fairness or something else. But fundamentalism can't listen to other dualities, because it's based on the idea that there is only one duality. It's fundamentalism against the darkness of unbelief. Fundamentalism can't listen to new ideas or ways of thinking and still be fundamentalism.

But that's not to say it is all bad. I think of it as a place I was at one time but now have left to move on. In some ways fundamentalism made me what I am today. It gave me a moral universe, a sense of service and a desire to be part of something larger than myself. There is still a part of me that says, *Maybe Christianity is true exactly the way they say it is. Or maybe it's not true at all.*

One of my memories from Bible camp is the speakers who would give the altar call: "Are you saved?" I didn't go down, but I usually got saved again just in case. I would pray the prayer all over again, just like I had done many times before. My thoughts at the time have always stuck with me: *I have already done that, but I'd better do it again just to be safe.*

As I got out of that self-contained world and began associating with other people who had other beliefs, I saw that there were many different ways to view life. But in a sense I already knew that.

After the fundamentalist teachings about sex and marriage, for instance, I was surprised to find out that women were as physical as I was. As a boy, I was taught that the members of the opposite sex were "women," as opposed to people, and there were certain things I couldn't do with them until I got married. It was a surprise to find out that they were as human and sexual as I was.

Again, I don't recall one big turning point in my thinking, but when I first lived with a woman it did seem like a big departure from my family and church friends. But that was just an outward manifestation of a change in my thinking that had been going on for some time.

6

If God Exists, & If He's Good, That's Enough

At fifty he has lived many lives: a missionary kid in occupied Japan, a marine in the early days of the U.S. buildup in Vietnam, and a would-be bohemian writer and filmmaker. As a disillusioned practical atheist, he returned to Japan to teach English. There he experienced savage spiritual warfare. His marriage to his childhood sweetheart broke apart and later was healed and restored, along with his faith in Christ.

Later on his wife died a painful death from cancer. He is now a single father struggling to raise his children. His writing career is finally on an upswing, beginning with a well-received play based on biblical characters and themes. He is deeply reflective, scholarly and soft-spoken, but has a keen sense of irony and humor. His voice is deep and resonant.

We sit under ripening fruit trees on a summer afternoon in the wicker chairs he favors when he writes. A Buechner novel sits next to his Bible on the low table. During the interview his young children, acting as waiters, take our orders for soft drinks and homemade cookies. The interview is frequently punctuated by children and an assortment of neighborhood dogs seeking someone to throw sticks. The dogs also try to filch the chocolate-chip cookies so tantalizingly arrayed on the snout-level wicker table.

Little green apples drop on us when the wind blows. A gray squirrel raids the vegetable garden, trying to haul off a potato that must weigh more than it does.

* * *

My parents came from the conservative branch of a very conservative denomination, but our group was somewhat less rigid than others. My dad told me how frightened he was as a child when he heard children being baptized in the bathtub. They had been sprinkled in another denomination, but now that the parents had found the true church, they had to baptize their kids in the true way. I guess there was a line of kids and babies waiting in the hall, all hearing the screams as the little ones were forced under. He thought they were being drowned.

That was odd, really, because we believed in baptism only after a child had made a public declaration of faith. It was a mishmash of a couple of traditions. I don't remember those rebaptisms happening when I was a boy.

We had no formal clergy, just a meeting where we sat in a circle and waited for the Spirit to move the elders to speak. The elders weren't formally named, so nobody actually knew for sure who was an elder. We were supposed to know who was a true elder through the Spirit. If people had appointed them, it might not be of God, you see. If you were living in the Spirit, you would know. If you were backslidden, you might not be so sure.

I went to those meetings every Sunday morning, Sunday evening and Wednesday evening for the first nine years of my life. I sat in the same chair watching my feet dangle, waiting for my legs to grow long enough for my feet to touch the floor, as the same men said the same things week after week. Women were not permitted to speak. In fact, among the requirements for membership was that a wife cover her head, remain silent and show evidence of submission to her husband.

The elements, as we called them, were covered on a table until it was time for Communion. Beforehand we always sang—*he sings*—"Man of Sorrows, what a name / For the Son of God who came . . ." and I could smell that grape juice and the yeasty bread under the cloth. I never partook, because we left for the mission field in Japan before I came "of age." In a sense I miss having that experience for my kids. Their experience of church is framed by the many yuppies who attend: "Let's all have fun!" I'm beginning to understand the value of rituals.

After the war General Douglas MacArthur called for a thousand missionaries. He said that the only way the Japanese would come around was through the Christian gospel, not through politics. About four hundred answered the call, and we were among them. The Japanese were hated and reviled in America at that time, so those who went were real zealots. Once in Japan, we were no longer in that tight little cloister. We were now among an amalgam of very conservative Christians from many denominations.

All six siblings in our family went to the missionary boarding school, which I thought was wonderful because I could get away with so much. Compared to my father, the schoolteachers were downright lenient, although they were very strict fundamentalists.

In chapel we had speakers like Corrie ten Boom, and that was very inspiring. The Air Force band came once and, probably because we were Christians, played "When the Saints Go Marching In." The parents were coming to pick us up for the weekend, and I remember vividly the reaction of one of the mothers when she heard the band blowing that jazzy New Orleans rendition. She raised her hands heavenward, yelling, "Oh Jesus, have mercy on us! Stop up our ears!"

How did you feel about her reaction at the time?

He laughs heartily. Oh, I just thought, *What a dork!* But I knew what was expected of me, so I didn't let on what I thought.

We had devotions every day at school, and on Saturday we had devotions all morning with the family. And I'm glad for it, although I wasn't at the time. My dad approached devotions in a very rote way that bored me to death, so I vowed that I would never have boring devotions when I had a family. I got so bored once that I refused to sing a song that we always sang. My rebellion was telling my dad that I couldn't remember the words. So he said, "Okay, then you can just sit here until you can remember." The other kids went out to play, and I got so frustrated, I really couldn't remember the words. I tried to sneak a look in the hymnbook, and my dad caught me. I remember him peering around the corner, stealing a peek at me.

So how did you keep devotions from getting boring for your kids?

I told stories. When they were young we would even act out the Bible stories. I think it worked.

As a kid I rebelled, but I always feared God. I didn't learn to love him until much, much later in my life. My dad and I had a falling-out several years ago. I forbade him to come to my house because he kept instilling that same fear in my kids. He was putting them in the same mode of guilt and dread that I grew up in.

I remember him locking me in a dark closet when I was very young. I was terrified. And it was all in the name of learning to fear God.

I now consider my father a truly great man, but it took me until I was nearly fifty to understand him. After I banished him, we had a big family meeting. My brothers came from far and wide. One flew in from Japan. When I explained my decision, my father kept repeating over and over: "I just don't understand this need to *feel.* When I was young we just tried to *live.*"

My dad never played as a child, because he had to work to help his family get through the Great Depression. When I saw the connection between his childhood and his inability to feel emotion, I understood for the first time that he was a lonely boy who couldn't form relationships with other people. Six months later I wrote a letter to him that recalled some of my favorable memories of him. My mom called me and said tearfully, "I have my husband back." He had gone into a deep depression when I banished him from my home. It just caught him completely off balance—he didn't even know what he had done.

I had thought all my life that he had no feelings. He had always been so stern, so unbending, that I thought he could endure anything, but he couldn't take my anger or rejection. He told my brother that he was afraid of me! It had never occurred to me that my dad could be afraid or hurt by anything, let alone me.

"A good name is to be desired more than much fine gold." That was one of Dad's favorite verses, and we heard it a lot. I was the only one of the six kids who rebelled, and when I finally came back as an adult it gave my dad great pleasure. So many of the kids in our congregation went wild or astray. Some became criminals. One girl just took off into the woods, and we figured someone had murdered her. A lot of them had multiple marriages and divorces. Dad would see the devastated families and take great pleasure that his six kids were walking with the Lord as adults.

I became a practical atheist as a young adult, declaring that God existed but acting as though he didn't. I married a girl from the mission school who had been as rebellious as me. When the teachers heard about it they said, "You deserve each other."

I went to a very conservative Bible school in the Midwest, and one of the things we preacher boys had to do was start a church in a rural area. Ours had fewer than fifty people, and we met in an abandoned Lutheran church building that was falling to pieces. We visited people to enlist them. One farmer ran us off his land at gunpoint. We all wrote that in our diaries! We were proud to have been persecuted for Jesus' name's sake.

I was so young. My biggest problems were in my thought life. I would see a farm girl walking down the road in her tight blue jeans and then teach Sunday school while my mind was filled with raging lust. To have the thought was to commit the deed, so I lived in a perpetual state of sexual arousal and guilt. But I couldn't talk about it. I just taught Sunday school and felt like the biggest hypocrite in the world.

I was drafted shortly after that, and although I didn't want to go into any branch of the armed forces, I figured I might as well have a challenge, so I enlisted in the Marines. The recruiter asked me, "Will you kill for us?" I said I didn't know. He told me that I had an hour to think about it and decide if I could kill for the Corps. This is one of the areas where all that religious training left me high and dry. I didn't know how to approach the question. I figured that if I was drafted into the Army, I might have to kill. Therefore I might as well kill in the Marines. So I went back and told the sergeant, "I suppose I could kill if I had to." And then I joined the Marines.

I was in one of the first big amphibious landings at Pleiku. We climbed down ratlines and into the landing craft just like in the movies. It was a great adventure. Then the bullets started pinging, and it wasn't so much fun. It was surreal. John Wayne visited us, and a sniper started shooting. He didn't know what all the pinging was, so a corporal tackled him to keep him from getting shot. Later on the guy who played the sergeant on *Gomer Pyle* arrived by helicopter, talked to us for a half an hour and then took off again. I also remember one USO show starring a famous dancer who, according to rumor, never wore panties. A guy with a camera crawled under the stage, which had wide spaces between the planks, and took pictures. He showed us prints later that he said were the genuine article. The whole time in Vietnam was strange.

I never killed anyone, although I was in some battles where people died on both sides. I saw dead people and counted bodies. I was so afraid of death that I tried to bribe God by staying as close to orthodoxy as I could. I don't think that I experienced the so-called delayed stress syndrome. I remember telling myself when I left Vietnam to remember that what I hated and feared most were the rats and mosquitoes. Too many guys came back and built up stories about battles and deeds that never actually happened.

It was after Vietnam that I became a practical atheist, saying that God existed but acting as though he didn't. My wife and I got jobs teaching conversational English at a private school in Japan, and I began to examine Buddhism and Zen. I hung out with a group of expatriates. One of my buddies was getting his black belt in karate. I wanted to write the great American novel, so I began hanging out in coffee shops, writing drivel. I couldn't write anything worthwhile because I was so closed, so confused. I felt that I didn't have anything to write about.

My wife finally left me and moved to the Japanese mainland. My friend John and I began hanging out more and more, both of us trying to be the next Hemingway. I was reading Gide and the existentialists.

And then the first of two defining events in my spiritual life occurred.

John and I decided one night to climb a mountain the following morning. He left on his motorcycle, and at 3:00 a.m. I heard someone banging on my door. I found a note that said, "John dead. He died in auto accident." I felt an overwhelming darkness that lasted three days, but it was the beginning of a long journey back to faith.

The next day I saw John's karate instructor walking down the road. He was dressed in black, including a black beret. He saw me and bowed, and when his head went down, the beret lowering to obscure his face was like an eye closing. I saw him later on a train and said, "John is . . . is . . ." I couldn't think of the Japanese word for *dead.* He smiled and said "John!" and made a karate chop. I said, "No, John," and made a slit throat sign. He thought I was agreeing that John was a great karate fighter and nodded his head, making more karate chops in the air. I couldn't make him understand.

I went to John's house and saw that it was draped in black and white banners, signifying death. I'll never forget that sight: a zebra across the shimmering green of the rice fields, growing larger and larger as I walked toward the house.

In the house were about fifteen female students on their knees. When I entered they immediately turned away from me. I thought I had done something wrong, but that is the custom—to let a man have his time of grief in private.

Normally they would have cremated him, but because he was a Catholic (cremation was prohibited by Catholic teaching), they packed him in dry ice instead. He had told me the day before that he was on top of the world. "I have my black belt, my teeth are all fixed, and Mariko is not pregnant."

Now the blood was discoloring his ears, and I could see where they had stitched up the wounds. The light glinted off a new filling in his open mouth. "What we do?" they kept asking me, pointing to the open box and the dry ice that was rapidly melting in the heat.

I felt like Huck Finn when he went to his own funeral. I kept seeing myself lying there in that box, and I was terrified by the specter of death in a way that I had never felt in Vietnam.

I went back to my house and read *Moby Dick* and said to myself, *It's 3:00 and I'm alive.* A few minutes later: *It's 3:03 p.m. and I'm alive.* I felt as though I was enclosed in a bell jar. On the third day—this will sound really weird—I saw three beings squatting in my room. I felt as though I was about to throw myself out the window. I looked at those beings and began to ask what their names were, but then I thought, *If you do that, you'll give them authority to enter you.* I was really on the edge. So finally I just shouted out, "Jesus saves!" and it was like something broke. *He laughs.* That's all I could think of to say.

The beings disappeared. I realized at that moment that I had called on God's name without asking if he existed. I thought, *That's enough. If God exists and he's good, that's enough. If you have known evil face to face, and God exists and he's good, why rebel? What's the point?*

I had to get out of Japan, because I felt overwhelmingly that I was in the middle of a spiritual battle. When I got back to the States, I almost fell down and kissed the earth.

I was still terrified of dying until one day in 1973, when a friend invited me to a charismatic meeting in a Catholic church. I went there to silently jeer at their antics, since I knew that Catholics were wrong. While I was there, the second defining event of my spiritual life occurred.

I don't tell people about this too much, because it sounds crazy. I was looking up at the ceiling of this grand cathedral, and the roof literally came off the building and clouds began rolling in. I saw a pair of enormous feet and heard the sound of angels singing, "Thou art worthy."

I stood there observing this in a scientific manner, thinking that everyone else was seeing the same thing. Then I wept and completely broke down. It was as though the Holy Spirit had been a block of ice all those years, and now he was streams of living water. I was so full of joy, I went out and began telling everyone I met. I told my neighbor, who is a university professor. That was a mistake. You can't just tell people about an experience like that.

That was the end of my association with my parents' church. They told me to leave. I began attending a charismatic church, which went against all the dogma of my upbringing. But that sense of overflowing joy filled and defined me for years.

I called my wife and told her I had changed, but she was pretty skeptical. It took another two years for her to trust me and come back. A year later she had a similar experience, and then we were really together. We went back to Japan as missionaries.

I was very apprehensive about going back to Japan because of the spiritual darkness I had suffered there. In the airport I had one of the strangest experiences of my life. I was waiting with the luggage when I saw a tall, dapper Caucasian. He walked over toward me, and I thought was going to greet me or ask me something, but instead he began screaming, sort of stuttering or babbling, "We don't want you here! We don't want you here! You smell! You smell! You smell!" He was ranting, almost foaming. Then I said, "In the name of Jesus . . ." and he turned and walked away, right through the customs gate.

Not an auspicious beginning, but the two years in Japan were the best two years of our lives. I was empowered by the experience in the Catholic church, and it defined me and colored my life for years.

What changed it?

My second marriage. My first wife died of cancer, and although that was tragic and sorrowful, I still had a sense of joy. But my second marriage just wore me down. She was a woman who almost celebrated doubt. That marriage was deeply troubled, and it just took the life out of me.

I'm still walking with Christ, but I haven't regained that euphoric sense of God's presence that I had during those last years with my first wife. I miss that.

We had a reunion of students from the missionary academy. There were students from a ten-year period spanning the mid-fifties to the mid-sixties. With one or two exceptions, all had left the faith and come back. And those of us who had come back had one thing in common: we had all discovered grace in our forties.

One guy had run with so many women and abused drugs and alcohol so heavily that he looked like he was seventy. There were a couple of people who left when we started talking about Jesus, but almost everyone had gone the same route I had traveled. One guy had been on the FBI's Ten Most Wanted List. He started to give a testimony about how he had finally given his life to Jesus last week, and we were all rejoicing, but his brother cut him off.

I said, "How come you won't let him finish?" He said, "He's still high from whatever it was he took a half an hour ago." He was pretty screwed up. I remember him as a fat, scary kid in school. I had seen him a few years earlier when he got out of prison, and he was lean and even scarier.

But for the rest of us, it was like being with brothers and sisters. We never fit into Japanese or American society. Our fundamentalist background had given us a sense of belonging *and* a sense of alienation, but we all came back to Christ.

Part 2

The Life of the Mind: Intellect, Heart & Soul

7

I Didn't Have to Untie All the Gordian Knots

He's a Vietnam veteran, a scholar and an author who has lived in Europe, Canada and the United States. He seems to know a great deal about everything without being pretentious. He's a carpenter, auto mechanic, computer whiz, musician and actor. He's also a gourmet and a fine cook.

He teaches in Christian colleges and writes for a number of Christian publications. He is active in an evangelical church, and he finds his faith in Christ to be the centerpoint of his life. His theology puts him in the company of Christians who are more socially and politically conservative than he is, and they have at times considered him "dangerously liberal," to quote one of his former administrators.

* * *

My father was a preacher in a very conservative wing of an extremely conservative denomination. We lived for many years in a garage that Dad was converting into a home. In retrospect it seems that the house was always in a state of construction, because Dad was gone so much. We never had much money, and I guess we saw that as part of being preacher's kids. Dad's preaching took him away from home, and when he was home he was pretty busy. My siblings still recoil in horror at the thought of home remodeling. They get nervous when they see me tearing my place up, because they are reminded of those lean, meager years in the garage.

Even though our church was very conservative, Dad felt that our denomination was too liberal, so we joined a very exclusive sect that tried to live as simply as possible. No drinking, smoking or dancing, of course. No jewelry or fancy clothes either. Nothing that hinted at aesthetic pleasure. Maybe *(he laughs)* that's why I enjoy a glass of brandy and a good cigar today.

We could only read books that were on The List, so when I had something I wanted to read, I kept it in my locker at school. I was always reading, because if I took a book home I knew that Dad would eventually pick it up and forbid me to read it.

Was there an actual list of books and authors?

No, but there were several authors of our theological bent that we were encouraged to read, and anything else was suspect. Fiction was not something worth a Christian's time, so it was mainly theology and devotional literature.

We lived in a small provincial town—my world was very enclosed in some ways. I did quite well in high school though, and I was fortunate to get a scholarship to a college in the Ivy League.

That was quite an eye-opener. I went from hearing the absolute final word on everything in a tiny congregation to hearing world-famous scholars expound on philosophy, literature and the arts. That experience can be very troubling for fundamentalist young people. You see those kids in college all the time. They come in and argue every point with you, insisting that they have "the truth."

Unfortunately, those kids are often completely unused to scholarly debate. They have always heard adults pronounce the final word. Many times their father, the preacher or the deacon has said, "This is how it is," and that's the end of it. In a university environment, where the debate is part of a conversation that has gone on for centuries, they fall pretty fast. I've seen many of them just give up and abandon their faith, or drop out of college.

For whatever reason, I didn't feel a need to win debates with professors. My faith was very real to me, although I did have many questions about the oversimplified worldview of our church.

Many, many times I would read or hear something that seemed to blow the Christian faith out of the water. That happened especially when I studied history and saw the failures of the church throughout the centuries. And in philosophy and anthropology I was faced with different, more informed opinions about why people behave the way they do.

That was in the fifties and sixties, when modernism and relativism were really taking hold in the universities. I learned to just table some issues and come back to them later. I didn't feel that, as a teenager, I had to be able to untie all the Gordian knots. I got more information, thought and prayed, read, and eventually I was able to reconcile questions that seemed too difficult to me at first glance.

How were you able to develop the critical thinking skills that helped you remain faithful in academia?

I suspect that it really began with my high-school debate team. Debate, at least in its formal manifestation, is much like what passes for discussion in some theological circles. You already know what viewpoint you are trying to champion, so you look for "facts" that will support your cause. You also look for facts and quotations that will destroy your opponent's argument.

As a young teenager I just accepted this, and often I would find an expert whose argument seemed to demolish my opponent's argument. I would write it down on a little 3 × 5 notecard and wait eagerly for the next debate.

The funny thing is that it rarely had the effect that I had anticipated. My opponent, if he was any good at all, would just pull out his counterargument.

I remember coming to a realization. It may have been in my senior year of high school, when I had exhaustively researched and debated both sides of that year's topic. I came to understand that no matter how strange or downright stupid your argument was, you could find a credentialed expert to support you. So even before I went to the university, I knew that you could have a Ph.D. and be a moron. For instance, look at all the scholars whose claim to fame is their championing of Marxism. Try to get a job with that perspective in Eastern Europe today. They will dismiss you as a fool.

I took that attitude to the university. When I listened to a lecture, I would think to myself, "This professor has a Ph.D. and the acclaim of the academic world. He's published books, advised governments—but he may be completely wrong." So I would listen respectfully and attentively, and then I would sit on it for a while. I soon found that the so-called devastating arguments against Christianity were not really so devastating after you had understood them completely. Many of them (again, some of the Marxist-oriented ones) have been defused after less than a century. Meanwhile, the church thrives after two millennia.

One thing the university helped me with, though, was to show me just how much of what is called Christian doctrine is simply the folkways of a particular group. And that's the part that scares some fundamentalists. The critical skills cut both ways. You see foolishness and sloppy thinking both inside and outside the faith.

Here's an example. In Canada we once had a conference of the Canadian and German branches of our church. I remember it very clearly. The Germans were appalled by the way the Canadian children squirmed and fidgeted all through the service. How could those Canadian parents call themselves believers when they couldn't control their own houses? The German kids sat bolt upright and were as silent as little cadavers.

Then we had a picnic, and the Germans lit up their pipes and poured their beer. The Canadians almost had a collective heart attack. How could those Germans really be Christians when they were drinking and smoking for all to see? And right there in front of the children! *He laughs.* The poor Canadians didn't even have the vocabulary to deal with it. There were Christians, and then there were people who smoked and drank. It was like trying to understand that someone was a Jewish Nazi. I watched all this and took it in.

Another time *(he grins widely)* a rather portly American came up to a European who was smoking after the meeting and pointed right at the offending cigarette while he asked in a mighty voice, "And what will your God say to you about *that* on Judgment Day?"

The European, who was quite tall and thin, took a deep drag, exhaled a huge cloud over the American's head and poked the American's rather distended belly. "What," he asked calmly, "will your God say to you about *that?"*

Neither of them said another word. The discussion had completely exhausted its possibilities. There was no room to maneuver. They probably both went home thinking exactly what they'd thought before they had come to the gathering.

I have to admit that it all seemed pretty silly to me when I compared it to the kinds of discussions I was having in college. College discussions were challenging. We would stay up late arguing about things that really mattered. In that Ivy League school there were plenty of students and professors who really wanted to know about things. Sometimes the Christians just seemed to recycle the same old truisms. It was tempting sometimes to dismiss Christians as bumpkins who just hadn't been out much.

In our second denomination particularly, a good meeting was one where someone presented an even more narrowly focused definition. A man would feel moved by the Spirit to explain predestination or the distinction between justification and propitiation. I couldn't help wondering how any of this was going to make us come closer to Christ in our actual lives. It was all geared toward doctrine.

I never lost my faith, but I had a time where it seemed less a part of my life. Then I went to Vietnam and saw real evil. That experience made me see more clearly the need for a Savior.

I also saw patterns of behavior in people. Some of the sergeants seemed a lot like the deacons in my church. They were very confident of their own rightness, even when they were dead wrong. I saw officers who couldn't learn from anyone they saw as their subordinate. They were in authority, therefore they were always right.

One new officer found an unexploded mortar shell that had landed on the perimeter of the camp, so he decided to have a couple of guys bury it. If he had asked anyone who had been in country for more than a couple of weeks, he would have left it for the ordinance disposal unit. Or if he'd even had a lick of common sense, he might have told everyone to stay clear of it. But he took two privates out there and ordered them to bury it. Those two privates went with him like sheep to the slaughter. The officer had spoken, so they followed. When they touched it, the mortar shell exploded and killed them.

I got very distrustful of people who had all the answers and no questions, or who felt that they knew everything about everything by virtue of who they were.

When my tour of duty was over, I was sent to a small coastal town to await a flight back to the States. Then I got the word that one of my sergeants had decided to take the desk jockeys (the clerks) out on a search-and-destroy mission. He was going to make sure that those sissies didn't spend all their time typing and filing. No sir!

Well, they ran right into a well-placed Vietcong ambush, and they were cut to pieces. Those clerks hadn't been out in the field, so they didn't really know how to dig in, communicate or even use their weapons effectively. The platoon was almost completely wiped out. Over a hundred guys, including every friend I ever had in Vietnam, were killed in a matter of a few minutes.

There I was, essentially sitting around in a resort town waiting to go home. I couldn't go to their funerals, comfort their families or anything. They were just gone. I was very disoriented and alone. I met three guys who were on R&R. They were pretty wild, drinking nonstop and burning the candle at both ends, but they took me in and were very kind to me. Somehow they knew that I needed companionship.

After we got talking, I found that they had gone through a very similar experience—walking into an ambush and losing most of their friends. They were younger than me, just teenagers, but there was a dark, deeply troubled manner under all the bravado. It turned out that after the fight they had been taking some Vietcong prisoners back to the base on a helicopter. They were so blinded by grief and hatred that they flew over a Vietcong area and threw the prisoners out at about five thousand feet. They talked it up, but I could see that they had gotten no joy from that experience, just a taste of evil that had really stained them.

Then I got on a plane for the States. A couple of weeks later I was teaching a class in U.S. history at a Christian school. That was a real jump from one world to another. The school had its fundamentalist core group, including a number of John Birchers. They immediately suspected that I was a communist sympathizer because of my Ivy League credentials and the fact that I was pretty ambivalent about Vietnam. Also I wore a beard—just like Trotsky! They held the view that the war was part of God's plan to defeat communism by any means necessary. By that time I saw the war for what it was: a terrible, cruel mistake.

Conservative Christians didn't want to talk about my experiences in the war or my doubts about the marriage of American jingoism and the gospel, so I just didn't talk about it much, except to other vets. I never cried for my dead friends until twenty years later, when I saw Oliver Stone's movie *Platoon,* which was very close to my experience. I went over to the home of a Christian friend who was also a vet, and we cried together.

In the true, historical sense of the word, I am a fundamentalist. I believe in the virgin birth, the authority and truth of Scripture, the bodily resurrection and the atonement. But I'm not a fundamentalist in the current usage of the word. I still have more questions than answers. That's why I need a Savior.

When did you actually break from your parents' exclusive fundamentalist sect and enter the more mainstream evangelical church you attend now?

There was an actual moment, as it happens. Our theology was based on dispensationalism, which was something I could never truly fathom. My father, however, didn't stress dispensationalism all that much, so it was somewhat out of my mind.

I was about thirty at the time, married and well established in my teaching career. I was helping edit a magazine and attending a lot of seminars in the larger Christian church. I knew a lot of people who had different views.

We had another conference, like the one with the beer-drinking Germans I mentioned earlier. It was a week-long retreat, and the main speaker focused exclusively on dispensationalism. Suddenly I said to myself, *I do not, cannot believe this.*

I wrote a long letter to my father in which I said that I did not believe that the Bible was meant to be a cosmic jigsaw puzzle. I also said that as a Reformational believer, I couldn't accept a theology that could only be understood with the assistance of the Scofield Reference Bible. I came to believe that the human desire to systematize the Bible—God's holy, living Word—within a prefabricated structure was to ignore its truth and the work of the Holy Spirit.

He didn't take that too well, and that church really couldn't be a place for me anymore. It caused great hurt, which hasn't completely disappeared after twenty years. I think my folks still think of me as a boy who has gone astray. Of course, none of my siblings stayed in fundamentalism either, although they are all active Christians.

Systematic theology is pretty near and dear to most fundamentalists and evangelicals. How do you interpret the Scriptures without a system of some kind?

In my relationships with Christian students I try to live and explain the Christian faith without necessarily agreeing with all the myriad rules that are causing them to doubt. Sometimes that gets me in trouble with more conservative Christians, but I've never had an alumnus come back and criticize me for being too open. I do know of some who have later criticized teachers for being too protective of them, though. I try to give my students what I needed when I was in their shoes. I think that Christ redeems our experiences, so even though some of the disillusioning experiences of college and Vietnam were not in themselves good ones, they can be used to the glory of God.

So I expect my students to doubt, to question and even to rebel a bit. I try to help them find Christ through their school experience.

8

Nudes, Cadavers & a Nine-Hundred-Foot Jesus

He's an artist and a middle-aged father. He directs an evangelical student ministry on one of America's largest university campuses. His organization requires its staff members to have a strong background in an academic discipline as well as a knowledge of Scripture and doctrine.

We meet in a coffeehouse one block away from the campus. It is situated in a bohemian neighborhood that was once a favorite haunt of beat poets and, later, the hippies of the sixties. The area has retained a certain bohemian flavor, although it's mostly populated by achievement-oriented business and engineering majors who are the real movers and shakers now.

* * *

I was always interested in art, which made me a bit suspect in our particular church. Art and artists were somehow decadent. Our church was made up of good Midwestern families who ate meat and potatoes and drove Chevrolets and Fords.

I wasn't trying to be subversive, but my interest in art, movies, painting, poetry and literature didn't give me much common ground with the people in the church. It was hard in a way, because I was a serious Christian, but when I talked to people about art it was as though I was backsliding.

How did your parents feel about your interest in art?

They weren't crazy about my becoming an artist, but they didn't lay the guilt trip on me like some of the other adults did. I think they felt like they had raised me the best they knew how, and they trusted the Lord to guide me in my life. Even if I was going to be a painter *(he laughs).*

I went to a state university, and that was a culture shock. The other art majors were into all the trendy philosophies and art movements. There were expressionists, neorealists, abstractionists and all that. I didn't feel the need to jump on one of those bandwagons, so I tried to learn from everyone and everything.

The subject matter of art was very different in the university from what it was in church. Most of the people I knew thought that art was either something pretty to put over the fireplace or something affirming—like a picture of praying hands, or a nine-hundred-foot Jesus standing next to the United Nations building. In other words, art was something that was so obvious in its meaning that you couldn't possibly miss the point.

But art in the university was like literature. It pushed the boundaries and asked questions that couldn't be answered in a simple way. I learned to appreciate the fact that artists were not just decorators. I read some of Francis Schaeffer's writing about art, and Hans Rookmaker's. It helped me see that there were Christians who knew and respected art.

So then I started to build my own skill. We did all the basic classes in painting, sculpture and so forth. Then we drew nudes, which is where all artists have to start. I wondered if that was going to be arousing, but it really wasn't.

A Christian college in my city paints the human figure wearing a bathing suit. They don't feel that you have to have nude models to get the basics.

I would have to respectfully disagree. In our society we automatically associate nudity with sex, thanks to skin magazines and television ads. We have learned that the body is a means to titillation. I think that most people go into their first figure class with some of those notions.

But you get over all that stuff after the first round, that first shock when you discover that other bodies are very much like the one you have. It's different from the locker-room experience, in that you are permitted a long gaze. Where else do you get to look at a naked body for an extended period of time without a question attached? If you did that in the locker room, people would really wonder—you can give a passing glance, but not a prolonged gaze. So you go through the shock, but then eventually you begin to actually appreciate the body. When you draw it, it becomes like landscapes, like rocks . . . It becomes abstract, it becomes sensuous in a nontitillating way, though sometimes it still is that too. Which is not in itself so bad.

I don't think drawing nudes ever becomes casual, and I think it does communicate a certain respect. There is a certain kind of humanity that is present in that kind of drawing: That is another person. That is not me. It's not property. It's not a prop that you can move around like a clay pot or a vase of flowers or something. Certainly you pose models, but you wouldn't really think about touching them when you pose them. You would say, "Well, how about moving this way . . . ?"

I remember one time in one of my first classes we were doing charcoal drawings of a female model, and a guy started drawing the breasts and pubic area very dark and pronounced. They were very erotic in a way—except that he didn't draw well enough to really make them erotic. I felt embarrassed for him, looking at his drawing, because he wasn't drawing what was up there. He was drawing what he imagined a woman looked like. It was so clear. He didn't have it right. He wasn't looking—he couldn't have been. So he just darkened in the nipples and pubic hair. There were three points in his drawing, and everything else just faded away. An accomplished artist might have tried something like that to make a point, but not this guy. He just wasn't looking. He made clear what he really thought women were. It was very embarrassing, but I don't think he realized that he should have been embarrassed.

That was an important learning experience for me, but I probably couldn't explain that to the people in my old church. The Greeks were the first ones to represent the human form in a realistic, idealized way. That reflects their humanistic philosophy, but it also reflects the fact that we are made in God's image.

I don't mean that God has a body like mine. At least I don't think he does. But my body, and everyone else's, reflects the glory of God. It's not an ugly or obscene thing.

Anyway, most artists don't spend all their time representing nudes. Leonardo drew nudes, and he dissected cadavers to see how they were made. That knowledge, that appreciation then allows the artist to build a technique that can speak to people. After all, having a body is a big part of who we are. It is what carries us into this world, and when it wears out, we leave this world.

Besides being uncomfortable with nudes, why do you think that conservative Christians have such a problem with art?

I can only talk about my experience. In my church it was very important to be right and to have all the answers. Art, like literature or science, is about searching for answers. That seems to make some Christians nervous, because sometimes their answers are superficial, and real searching leads them to new, frightening conclusions. Art is not a status quo thing. Good art is against the status quo.

He pauses, sips his coffee and takes a moment to form his thoughts. I'm grateful to my church, though. I never went through any long dark night of the soul. I learned the gospel and the Scriptures in my little church, and that has always stayed with me. There has never been a point where I stopped being a Christian, or thought I had stopped. I had questions, but I stayed with my faith in Christ.

That's what I try to do in my ministry. Lots of Christian kids come to the university, and to excel in their field of study they have to look at things that were off-limits in church. Genetics, evolution, medical ethics, art and literature are all searchers' disciplines.

I was helped greatly by the organization that I work for now. They gave me fellowship with other searchers. If you really feel called to something that wasn't part of your church background, it can be pretty lonely. They helped me to see that I could be a Christian and an artist. I saw other students being Christian scientists, philosophers, doctors and lawyers. *He laughs heartily.* Yes, even lawyers. That was an essential part of my spiritual growth, so now I do the same work with today's students.

I try to help students put their faith and their intellect together. If that doesn't happen, one of them has to go. Often it's the faith that goes, especially if it seems shallow and naive in the light of university study.

I'm grateful to my folks because they didn't just parrot the party line to me. I knew that they were faithful Christians, yet they let me see that they could also think and have an open mind. So even though they stayed in a church that was too restrictive for me, I knew that they didn't necessarily expect me to do the same. They always wanted me to follow the Lord, not their particular denomination.

9

Sometimes I Avoid the Big Questions

He's a tall, muscular scientist in his thirties, an outdoorsman who runs marathons, scuba dives and rides his mountain bike. Lately he's been crewing on ocean sailboat races. Since graduating from a small Christian college a decade ago, he has lived in the tropics, earning a master's degree and a Ph.D. while doing what he likes to call "pure research" on agriculture, aquaculture and natural flora.

He's easygoing, with a quick smile and a friendly manner. He's also articulate and thoughtful. His passion is the state of the earth's biosystems, and he can talk intelligently about the essential role of sharks in the food chain while gleefully describing how he almost entered that food chain when a large school of tiger sharks invaded a reef where he was working. Later he tells me about the effects of typhoons on rain forests and describes the 130-mph winds that took his mountaintop lab away in a flutter of splintered wood and bent tin roofing.

We share a cool drink on a shady veranda under a blazing sun and talk about the role of faith and Christian community in the world of scientific research.

* * *

How am I doing spiritually? Well, that's an interesting question. I guess I would have to say that I still try to follow the moral teachings of Christianity, but as far as going to church and all that, I'm in a process of questioning that is pretty hard. Sometimes I just avoid the big questions.

When I was in grade school we went to a church that I felt pretty good about, but then my folks decided that we needed to move to a charismatic church, and that was very hard for me. My parents seemed to feel that it was a step in the right direction, but I never fit in at all. I felt that I was marked as a bad person there. I was encouraged, then pressured, to speak in tongues. I looked in the Bible and saw where it said that *some* would receive the gift of tongues. I told them that I had no problem with that but I didn't feel that I was one of the ones who had that gift and I wasn't about to sit around babbling to myself until I tricked myself into believing that I did have that gift.

I felt very awkward there, and I let my parents know it, but they made me go to that church all through high school. It's very hard to be in a really wild, holy-roller kind of church when you don't believe in it. A lot of kids felt that they were expected to act up and get all involved in the worship even if it seemed phony to them.

In our old church the worship was more subdued, and I could listen and participate at my own level without feeling that I was being forced into something.

When I went to a Christian college it was better. I could worship in a way that was more real to me, and the distance between me and my parents gave me something of a zone of privacy.

During my undergraduate days there was quite a lot of friction between my folks and me, but we got along okay. They still wanted a speaking-in-tongues kind of response from me, though. It was supposed to be a freeing experience, but it was expressed in quite legalistic terms. I think that they hoped to protect me from liberalism by pumping me full of the Holy Spirit.

Things got more tense when I started doing graduate work in science. I was an assistant teacher, so I was criticized by people in the church for teaching evolution. "How can you teach that garbage?" they would demand. (Not my parents so much, but other people from the church.) It was hard to accept because these were people who had little or no understanding about science. But they knew that any teaching of evolution was unchristian.

I just didn't feel that way at all. The creation account isn't meant to be a science book. It's only a couple of pages long. I see it as a general description of the phases of creation. It seems to be very accurate to me if you think of the days as phases.

I would ask them, "Do you really think that the world is exactly as it was when God made it? Static? Couldn't God be creative enough to make a dynamic universe?" That is a much more exciting idea to me. Why make a universe that just stays the same? I don't mean dynamic as though he just made it and then wound it up like a clock either. That's just another form of static.

How so?

Either position reduces God to an automaton and his creation to some big clockwork. I see God as a living being.

Why couldn't God have made a world that changed through interrelation? People change. Countries change and evolve. But the church people just denounced me.

I don't know why they have to be so close-minded and judgmental. I don't mean to put myself above them, but I have a lot of experience, and not just out of books, either. I have studied ancient air trapped in a glacial ice bubble and examined it for trace elements. I have traveled around the world and studied the plants and animals. They're all interrelated! There is so much information, so many questions that the people in the church weren't even aware of.

I guess at this point I'm something of an agnostic, but I absolutely believe that the cosmos was created. It's just too complex and wonderful to be an accident. I don't know any scientists who are atheists on this point. They all seem to believe, based on their own observations, that there is a plan.

Well, maybe some physicists and mathematicians are atheists. They sometimes see the world in terms of mathematical probabilities. All of us scientists use that language to describe and analyze phenomena, but we see past the sterile idea that we're all here because of random happenstance.

When I talk to my colleagues, I share that belief with them. But we also have a hard time with the idea that God is just some old Jewish guy in a bejeweled chair. When Christians go on and on about science, I wonder: *Is this a Middle Eastern religion, or a European version of a Middle Eastern religion, that this person is giving me?*

A lot of the people I work with come from other religions—Buddhist, Hindu, Muslim—and we seem to share pretty much the same moral views. But all of us seem to have trouble with the simplistic, anti-intellectual forms of our religious backgrounds. That makes us wonder if it's just a personality trait that makes some people want to take their religion and put it in a static state. It may have little to do with revealed truth or faith. Maybe it's just a universal phenomenon that cuts across all cultures and religions.

You said that sometimes you avoid thinking about the big questions. Can you elaborate on that? It seems like you have given a great deal of thought to the big questions.

Like I said, I had some real difficulties with my father when I was young. I had some problems with my family, Pentecostalism, fundamentalism and Christianity. It's all sort of mixed together. I felt that if people in the church were going to make all these absolute statements, there should be evidence in their lives to back up the claims. They were saying that life was all planned out and if you did what they said, your life would be, in essence, better than other people's lives. But I didn't see much evidence to support that claim.

My parents' marriage was not without its troubles. There was a guy named Frank who chased after my mother for years. I guess she finally decided that there was something better out there, so she divorced my dad.

Strangely enough, my mother seems to be getting even more

conservative as she gets older. My father, on the other hand, was getting more liberal, or at least more open and tolerant. He and I were getting to the point where we could really begin to talk. He didn't have to be the guy with all the answers.

I was working hard to get my grant project done, and my dad and I were going to go sailing together as soon as I wrapped things up. Just him and me. We were finally going to have two weeks together to just reconnect. Then he died of a heart attack. That was shortly after my mom divorced him. I can't understand why we couldn't have had those two weeks.

I'm going home in a few weeks to see my family, but I'm not looking forward to it. Mom wants me to meet this Frank guy and get to know him. I don't want to meet him. I don't like him. *He laughs derisively.* I have a real hard time with the idea of talking to him because he did something very immoral that I would *never* do. I would never chase after someone's wife like that. Why should I meet him?

Is your mother still active in her church? Would you still consider her an active Christian?

Oh yes! That's part of my problem with formal religion. I just don't see how it all ties together. I don't know if this Frank guy calls himself a Christian or not. I don't care. Well, maybe I do care. I guess that's one of the reasons I sometimes just try to avoid dealing with the big questions. I don't like where they seem to lead.

I would like to believe that there is a way that God lives in people, but maybe if I really search it out, I will find out that he doesn't. I would prefer to keep that one open.

10

They Jump on Bandwagons

He's a very funny guy. His humor is quick and satiric, but not sarcastic. He is unusually well-read for a man in his twenties. His grasp of current events, politics and trends is buttressed by a strong background in history and philosophy.

After graduating from a Christian high school in the United States, he moved to Europe and studied first at an American university, then at a German-language university.

He has lived through the last days of communism, the end of the Berlin Wall and the breakaway of the former Soviet satellites. During those turbulent, heady times he traveled widely through Eastern Europe. He now lives with his girlfriend in an Eastern European capital city. They both speak several languages and make use of them in their conversation with one another.

* * *

I don't really consider myself a Christian anymore. In most European countries there are two churches, the Catholic and the Protestant. When people call themselves Protestants they really mean that they are culturally Protestant. The churches are organized and official and part of their heritage. Oh, there are some fundamentalist, Pentecostal and evangelical churches too, but they're pretty small and not really very influential. A lot of people see them as American transplants.

I was raised in an evangelical church, and I went to a private Christian school through the twelfth grade. I was always trying to fit into the Christian culture, but it was a struggle for me. My parents were pretty open-minded, but most of my friends' parents were very pushy. Some of my friends would have to go to camps and retreats and rallies where they seemed to be brainwashed. They would come home and burn all their rock 'n' roll records. Then in a few weeks they would buy the same records over again. They didn't seem to have much personal ownership of their spiritual growth. It was imposed on them through these mandatory activities.

My family didn't push me like that, but there was some of that kind of influence. In the Christian school I felt like I was on the outs much of the time. All the way through high school I felt, as did my friends, that I was a Christian. Looking back now, much of it seems to have been motivated by guilt.

When I came to Europe I found that things were much more relaxed. Their view of sex is, to my way of thinking now, much more sane. I used to have these huge attacks of guilt whenever I had a sexual thought. I was sinning! Most Europeans see sex as something more natural. The same with drinking. Granted, you see alcoholics, but most people don't go through the big frat-boy drinking binges that Americans do. Some of my friends from the Christian school went pretty crazy when they could finally get their hands on alcohol: "Look at me! I have beer! I'm drinking!"

I visited Amsterdam recently and toured the red light district. It was very interesting. The area is very large, and as you walk through you see women in the windows of little booths advertising all kinds of sex. When a customer goes in they just close the blinds.

The funny thing is that the Dutch people I knew frowned on the red light district. They wouldn't ever go there themselves, but they felt that it should be legal for people who wanted it.

In the cafés in the red light district the menus advertise drugs. You can say, "Yes, give me a cup of coffee, and we'll share a bong of your best hashish." But when I was there the customers mostly seemed to be foreigners. The Americans and Japanese were the real standouts, although the Germans were really into the drugs too.

It's kind of funny, really. Dutch people never go there themselves, but they have to take out-of-town visitors to see the hookers and sex shows and drug cafés. They see it as a tacky tourist thing, like some faux Indian village in an American town.

At the beach the girls might take their tops off if they're with their friends, but usually the beach is sectioned off into areas where that's okay. Some beaches have a section for nude sunbathing too. Tourists from America go crazy thinking about it, but it gets to be normal. The attitude of openness is counterbalanced with an attitude of respect, though. A woman wouldn't go topless in an area where it wasn't okay. People can do as they wish, but they have to respect others in a way that Americans, especially Christians, have trouble understanding.

But that attitude of openness does have some advantages. The teen pregnancy rate seems to be much lower in Europe. Europeans see Americans and American Christians as pretty schizophrenic about sex. On the one hand American Christians fight sex education, which is a given over here, but then their kids strut around with tight dresses and high heels like a bunch of hookers. That's what some German kids who visited my Christian high school said. It was true. The German girls dressed in jeans and sweaters. They didn't shave their legs or wear makeup. Some of the American Christian girls were in heels and short dresses and were all made up like movie starlets. The Germans just didn't get it. I guess I don't get it either.

Politics is based on a similar ethic. In most countries we have many political parties, not just two, so you have to compromise. In the two-party system you end up just lying about what you believe, or not talking about it. In Europe each party articulates its position, but then they compromise to form coalitions.

Here in the U.S. we read about hate crimes, the wars in Bosnia and the travails of the former Soviet countries. That doesn't sound like a place that's built on compromise.

That's true. Europe is small. It would fit into the lower forty-eight states with room left over. If we sit in a café in Vienna and talk about the war in Bosnia, that's like someone in Chicago talking about a war in Virginia. With all that history and all those different cultures, there's a lot of age-old hatred. Europeans are very much colored by their history. That's why so many young Europeans shy away from any religion or political system that smacks of tribal thinking. They have seen what narrow thinking can do, and they want no part of it. They want to live and let live, and absolutist religions are contrary to that direction.

Living in Europe made me look at things very differently. I like the way Europeans will discuss ideas in-depth. Americans, to me at least, seem more superficial, especially American Christians. They want to know who is the good guy and who is the bad guy, or what is the right way and what is the wrong way. Europeans tend to view issues on a continuum.

Is that really a better way? You seem to be saying that morality is just a matter of preference.

Well, yes and no. Americans, particularly Christians, like to find the problem and fix it. If something is right, do it. If something is wrong, don't do it. That I like. All this European moral ambiguity can get pretty frustrating. They can just sit around discussing a thing to death. On the other hand, the way American Christians jump on bandwagons without thinking the issues through is pretty frightening.

I follow the American press. During the Gulf War, Europeans were not so sure that the Kuwaiti royal family was a whole lot better than Saddam. But Christians in America seemed ready to invade and bomb a country that many of them knew nothing about. I wondered if more time would have softened Saddam's position. Then I saw that footage where the American bulldozers were just burying the Iraqi soldiers alive in their bunkers. Why don't Christians worry about the morality of things like that? Was that really the only way? If the Germans or

Russians had done something like that, it would have been seen much differently, but American Christians seem to see American foreign policy as an arm of God's will.

So much of what passes for Christianity in America seems to be based on middle-class suburban values. When I saw how much bigger and more complex the world was, I had a hard time with the easy answers I was given as a child.

In my Christian school, though, I had some teachers who tried to deal with the kinds of questions that I'm facing right now. I sensed that they got a lot of flak for it, though. I was just a kid, but I sensed that their lives would have been easier if they had just stuck to the easy answers. Those teachers seemed to care about me. It might have been because it was a small school, but I think that their concern had a lot to do with their Christianity.

So at this point I consider myself an agnostic. It's not that I have a big bone to pick with Christianity, it's just that it hasn't been convincing to me. It has its good and bad points.

I still try to live by the Christian ethical code, but then my best friend here is a Persian and he believes pretty much the same things as I do, or as my Catholic friends do. So if the moral codes are pretty much the same, what's the big deal?

11

Veering off the Sawdust Trail

He has spent a long morning teaching in a hot classroom, and he's ready for a break. His scholarly, professorial bearing is more like New England than Deep South, but he was raised on the "sawdust trail" of Southern revivalist fundamentalism.

Now a priest in a liturgical Protestant denomination, he wears the Roman collar that would have marked him as a heretic in his home church.

As we speak he chooses his words carefully, yet he has the academic's love of a free-ranging discussion and is willing to try on ideas. Despite his willingness to examine any theory or idea, he holds strongly to orthodox doctrines and beliefs.

We meet for a long lunch in an air-conditioned restaurant, where he loosens his collar and leans back in his chair. We spend several hours, often wandering far from the topic, yet always returning to it eventually.

When we part we are exhausted, yet energized, as though we had just played an afternoon of squash or tennis. He's not a man who could live with easy answers.

* * *

The early fundamentalists, the people who wrote The Fundamentals, were notable scholars of their time. They weren't just a bunch of yokels. If you go back and read what they wrote, it was very respectable theology. What happened to fundamentalism after that is a shame. It became very emotion-oriented and also very humanistic.

Most fundamentalists would take issue with you if you called them humanistic. Humanism is their sworn enemy.

I know. I don't mean to be divisive, but look at the way fundamentalist services are conducted. They aren't about worshiping God so much as they are an appeal to the man in the pew. The whole point is to elicit an emotion-based response, so you get the lowered lights, the soft music—all aimed at the people rather than at God.

That's an interesting interpretation, but isn't the idea to draw the person in the pew toward God?

That's the stated purpose, and it's probably an honest one, but when you cut yourself off from the Christian tradition and act as though Christ's church, for all practical purposes, began in America around 1901 or so, you don't have much of a blueprint to work from.

What we call fundamentalism (and I'm sure that you've had to deal with the problem of labeling this whole group) is really a product of revivalism, which is a separate theological tradition in many ways. Back in the nineteenth century the revivalist preachers would travel around, setting up their tents and preaching the sawdust trail. Down in front they would have what they called the "anxious bench," where sinners who were thinking about being saved could sit. When they got ready they would jump up at the altar call. The appeal was largely a hellfire-and-brimstone approach that said, "You'd better come right down here now or you'll burn in hell forever." It was extremely emotional and experiential.

That's why you get all these altar calls in fundamentalist churches today. Think about it. You have maybe a hundred or so people in the church service. Maybe half of them are at least fifty years old, and they have heard this same message every week for their whole lives. Yet three times a week they hear it again: "Come down and get saved."

Revivalist preachers would point out that sometimes there are people in the church who aren't saved and that the altar call also reaches people who are visiting.

That's true, but there's much more to the gospel than three altar calls a week for your whole life. I grew up in that kind of a tradition, and it was suffocating. Everything was oriented toward winning converts, so you couldn't raise any questions. I lived in a large city, and we would get these preachers from the boondocks of Mississippi or Louisiana who figured they had really arrived when they stepped into a pulpit in the big city. But they only had one essential message, and they didn't really know the Scriptures very well.

You really are stepping on toes here. Fundamentalists pride themselves in being Bible-believing Christians first and foremost.

True, but they don't really *read* the Bible. There's a tendency to pull a verse out here and there. Then when inerrancy became a pivotal issue, it pushed them into saying that the whole Bible was literally true. I would agree in principle, but you still have to recognize that Hebrew poetry, for example, isn't meant to be read as a science textbook. The Song of Solomon, for instance, is a poetic celebration of a man's love for a woman and vice versa. Fundamentalists get really nervous when they try to fit it into their dispensationalist shoebox. I heard a sermon where one breast was the Old Testament, the other was the New Testament, and the cleavage was the in-between time. Boy! You would never come up with that yourself. You only get interpretations like that when you're trying to squeeze the Scriptures into what you want them to say.

When you are raised like that, you can feel like the rug has been pulled out from under you when you start to ask questions. I was a fairly serious Christian as a young person, then I went into the Navy and went wild. I remember one day reading James Michener's *Hawaii* and being disgusted with the whole downside of the missionary endeavor. I just said, "I don't want any part of this!" and I became a practical atheist. It was over that fast. I knew that book was fiction, but it was based on fact, and much of it echoed things that had frustrated me and drove me crazy in church.

What brought you back?

To his credit, our pastor spent time with me and basically loved me back into the church. He wasn't able to address my most troubling questions, but he ushered me back into fellowship.

It was an uneasy peace that I had made with God, because I didn't have any real convictions, yet I knew that God existed and that I was a Christian. There were so many things that just didn't ring true to me, yet I had no way to examine them. To question was to doubt, and that was bad. I now firmly believe that doubt is an essential part of a dynamic faith. True faith can't really exist without doubt. But back then it was faith *or* doubt.

What were the big questions for you?

Well, the usual ones about the nature of God and the nature of evil. But I also just saw a lot of doctrines that didn't seem to match up. The rapture, for instance, never quite rang true to me. There's some evidence that the doctrine of the rapture can be traced to a young girl's utterance at a revival meeting. When you study it, you begin to see that dispensationalism confuses the general resurrection at the end of history with the rapture. If you read the book of Revelation in the light of Old Testament prophecy, it makes a lot of sense, but if you just pull it out and try to fit it into current events without its Old Testament context and roots, you can get pretty paranoid.

I saw a bumper sticker yesterday that said, "Refuse the Mark." It had "666" in the middle of a bar code.

He laughs and shakes his head. That's exactly what I'm talking about. In Deuteronomy the Jews were told to write God's law on their hands, heads and doorposts. There are still some orthodox Jews who write the law on a little scroll and put it in a little leather pouch headband, but the idea was that you would think about God's law in your head, do it with your hands and live it in your house. It's a poetic metaphor. So the mark of the beast can be seen as a metaphor for those who will choose to do likewise with Satan's law.

I had a hard time with some of the wild theories we would hear preached in church, although that whole end-times fad wasn't all that popular when I was a kid. That really hit the mainstream in the seventies with Hal Lindsey's book *The Late Great Planet Earth.* Modern fundamentalism's lack of biblical and historical grounding makes it highly susceptible to fads. If it sounds good and draws a crowd, it gets added to fundamentalist dogma. Fundamentalism has changed more than most fundamentalists would like to admit. It's hardly the unchangeable, rock-hard doctrine that it's made out to be.

So what influenced you to move away from fundamentalist theology after your return to the faith?

I met a theology student at the university who liked to debate. He was like me in that way. Even when he didn't know what he was talking about he liked to argue, and he was much better prepared than I was. This guy was a Calvinist, and I would have written him off as a liberal, but he knew the Bible so well that I had to respect him. He forced me to read, and then I found that there was a much larger Christian history than I had been led to believe.

I liked to read history even before I found the Reformers. *He laughs.* Then it was all sixteenth century for me! I wanted to live in a dynamic church like the ones I read about. When I discovered Calvin and Luther, things began to make sense. I found that many of the questions that plagued me had been dealt with by people much smarter and much more faithful than me. Calvin gets a bum rap today, but he was a remarkable thinker. It was liberating to find out about him and other Reformers.

Now I'm not saying that I'm some great intellectual, because I'm not. I don't consider myself an intellectual at all, but I'm not stupid. I'm capable of reading basic history and theology, as are most people. Remember, I was so clueless that when this guy asked me what I knew about St. Augustine, I could only reply that it was the name of the Catholic school up the road *(he laughs heartily).*

You're not the first of my subjects to decry the lack of historical perspective in the fundamentalist church. Why do you think this is?

Again, I think that fundamentalism is at its heart quite modernistic and humanistic. It's very individualistic, focused on the single person and his response to God. It takes a basic Reformation idea, the universal priesthood of the believer, and overemphasizes it to the detriment of other doctrines. And it's also quite emotional.

When I would raise an intellectual issue in my church that could have been addressed in reference to the Reformers or the church fathers, they would make an emotional appeal. When I questioned my salvation, the pastor told me to remember how I felt when I first asked Christ into my heart. Didn't I feel as though a great weight had been lifted from me?

That held me in check somewhat, but I knew that lots of things could make a person feel that a weight had been lifted off of them. Paying taxes and getting a refund, for instance. That's not a very good answer. At least it wasn't for me, and it isn't for a great many people.

The emotional appeal will do nothing at all for large segments of society. The Reformers, particularly Calvin, taught me that you could have a Christ-centered worldview as opposed to an experiential worldview. If you just try to build your faith on experiencing good feelings, you will run out of gas pretty fast.

The liturgical denomination in which you are ordained has some close affinities with Catholicism. How did you get where you are from your Calvinist stage?

Well, Calvinism, or the Reformed tradition, if you will, can be pretty austere. In some ways it was a reaction, like fundamentalism was. The fundamentalists reacted against German higher criticism and a liberal trend in the church. The Reformers reacted against the Roman church and its excesses. Whenever you react, you run the risk of throwing out some of the good with the bad.

I was in a Reformed church, but I read things in the Bible that made me question the way we worshiped. In Acts the early believers celebrated Communion every week, but we made a point of doing it once a month. I began to ask myself what worship might have looked like in the early church. I figured that it wouldn't be the freewheeling, entertainment-style service that is so prevalent today, nor would it be a dour bunch of people in a sterile building listening to lectures.

I began to read the church fathers, the people who led the church in the first few centuries, and found an incredibly rich worship system. Worshiping God was very important back then, and believers put their creativity, as well as their intellect, into it.

Puritanism went too far in paring down the church. The bare walls and the lack of instrumental music were a reaction against Roman Catholic ritual and pageantry. The Puritans stressed "regulative" worship: only that which was specified in Scripture was acceptable. Anything beyond that was "will" worship.

That Puritan legacy is very much a part of fundamentalism. The Puritan ethic is supposedly based on denying one's own will and seeking God's, but it often becomes its own kind of individualism. They wanted to nail everything down to a formula, even if the formula wasn't consistent with itself.

I have a theory on this, and it's completely untested. I don't even know if I want to have it written down in print.

Go for it. No one will confuse this book with systematic theology.

Okay. Well, I think that most people are personality types looking for theological justification. In other words, much of what we call theology is created to put God's stamp of approval on what we already believe, or what we need because of our personality type.

Some people need order, so they create a theology that makes everything concrete and predetermined. Some people want the freedom of inquiry, so they build a theology for it. Emotional people who need direct access to God create a theology where they can prophesy and receive words of wisdom.

But then I have to ask myself, If this is true, then is my theology just based on my personality type?

Isn't it possible that God allows people with different personalities to experience him in different ways?

Probably. But if we get too comfortable with our theology or too convinced of our absolute correctness, we are probably way off the track. That was what drove me crazy about fundamentalism. It convinced people of their absolute rightness when any fool could see the holes in their theories.

For instance, fundamentalists will laugh at the idea of Communion being a channel of God's grace. They completely reject the idea that any physical object, like bread or wine, could have any spiritual value. Yet the same people will tell you that you should never buy a troll doll or touch a ouija board, because they contain evil. In other words, God can't be in an object, but Satan can.

That's interesting. You're saying that there are two mutually exclusive theologies within fundamentalism. One for God and the other for Satan.

You could put it that way. Some fundamentalists don't drink, so they say that alcohol is inherently evil—the devil's brew. Yet the wine and bread have no part of God in them. If a person drinks a beer, he is communing with Satan. But Christian Communion doesn't exist. The bread and wine are mere symbols. If you grow up in fundamentalism, you notice inconsistencies like that. When you get out in the world you find that people see through you pretty fast, and you feel duped.

The fatal flaw in fundamentalism, I think, is individualism. It's not accountable to Scripture or history. You go to church and hear this list of completely arbitrary rules for living. But the rules are chosen—sometimes from Scripture, sometimes from the culture—to fit the group's prebiblical beliefs.

Can you define "prebiblical"?

Maybe that's not the right word, but what I mean by prebiblical is what we believe before reading the Bible. For instance, in the South when I was growing up they actually had armed guards at the doors of the church to keep black people out. *He laughs painfully.* As if any black Christian would want to come to a crazy racist church with gun-toting white deacons at the door. But the list of sins—drinking, gambling, dancing—was all based on individual behavior, as though the sinner didn't live in a culture that might be sinful.

That's where Reformation theology helped me. They saw that while a person could commit sin and be redeemed, a culture could also be sinful and in need of redemption. In the South we could be completely blind to the terrible racism that we were, to some degree, all a part of and benefiting from. A person could strive to live a pure and holy life without ever once considering the terrible sinfulness of the culture.

Maybe that's why white Christians still say that they didn't own slaves, therefore they aren't to blame for the racial problems of today.

Sure. We don't see our role in the culture. If we didn't personally own slaves, then it's not our problem. But that's not the way God spoke to the Israelites through the prophets. God doesn't only redeem individuals, he also redeems cultures. That's why Amos goes on and on about the sins of Sodom and Gomorrah, or why Jeremiah laments over Israel's unfaithfulness. They were calling the culture back to God.

I'm no legalist, but I do believe that God's law provides a model for our sanctification. If we read the Bible, however, we see that the law applies not only to personal actions but also to the culture in which we live. We're responsible for the culture too, regardless of whether or not we commit specific sinful acts.

But aren't modern fundamentalists like Jerry Falwell moving in the direction of civic responsibility?

In a way, but they still focus on personal sins that offend them and not on the overall sinfulness of the institutions in our society. It's still a very arbitrary list of sins.

Fundamentalists are very big on family values these days, but fundamentalist theology effectively excommunicates children from the church. In our church we baptize children because, as the children of believers, they share in grace. Fundamentalism doesn't allow children to share in grace, so they have to preach at them. The assumption is that the child is outside of Christ's church.

I believe that the child should get the benefit of the doubt. Then you don't have to spend all your time haranguing the child to get saved. You can teach and equip the child in ways that I wasn't. It's a sad commentary when kids know that something is wrong with the program, but they are merely encouraged to fall back on emotion. The church is almost two thousand years old, and it has had its share of triumphs as well as failures. We have to learn from that.

12

Mao, the Ivy League & Black People Who Like Rush Limbaugh

Her flashing smile and quick wit hint that she has a particularly sharp mind. She's considerably educated and well-read, yet this transplanted Northerner seems at ease in the laid-back atmosphere of tobacco country.

It's oppressively hot, and she and her husband have been painting the interior of their house. They have just moved here from the Mississippi Delta, where it was even hotter.

When I first ask to interview her, she isn't sure. Not out of any embarrassment about the details of her life, but because she's discovered the rich art of Southern storytelling. She feels that anything that comes out of her Northern mouth will sound bland and boring.

We chat awhile, sharing our enthusiasm for Southern writers and storytellers. She wasn't sure about moving to the South when she married, but now she feels that it has enriched and broadened her. She is surprised, in a way, that she has gained a deeper appreciation for her fundamentalist roots while living in the Bible Belt.

* * *

I was raised in a small fundamentalist, evangelical church that was mostly Asian-American. I also graduated from a small Christian school that I had attended since grade school. Most of my classmates went to Christian colleges, but I was accepted to an Ivy League university on the East Coast.

When I got to college I was blown out of the water intellectually. I had always been assured that the Bible was the holy book, but then I was thrown into an environment where few people accepted that idea at all. It was just stunning to be with all these professors, some of whom were world-famous writers and scholars, who could pick apart my cherished doctrines. I didn't know how to respond. It seemed that the Christian worldview I had accepted as unquestioned truth was just one of many ideas, and not a very well-reasoned one at that. The Judeo-Christian ethic, which had been taught to me as the true way, was just another philosophical construct.

I had no training in examining the Bible in light of history, dating or authorship, so I couldn't respond to the criticisms and attacks it was subjected to. I felt like William Jennings Bryan at the Scopes trials. I didn't want to throw away my faith, but it seemed that Christianity, especially fundamentalist and evangelical Christianity, was beaten—it was just an old philosophy in its final death throes.

And like any teenager, I had some problems with church and Christianity in general.

What kinds of problems?

Too much emphasis on witnessing and not enough concern for the poor and the oppressed. I didn't like the male authority structure of fundamentalism, or the anti-intellectualism. There was an arrogance that bothered me, a sense that white middle-class Christianity was the only way and that everyone else was going nowhere. Also, there was a certain amount of hypocrisy in my church and my school, so I started looking around at other value systems. I became interested in issues of justice and liberation.

In the early eighties the war in El Salvador was a big issue, so I got involved in a support group. It was made up of all kinds of people but was heavily populated by left-of-left types, including some Maoists. This was before the fall of communism in Europe and the massacre at Tiananmen Square. Those people spoke about liberation and freedom, but they were the hardest, most distrustful, most unloving people I had ever met. That made me reexamine my critical attitudes about my church to some degree.

It's true that Christians can be unloving, but they have no monopoly on it. Anybody can talk about love and not live it. I saw a lot more love in my church than I saw in those leftist liberation groups.

I also got involved in the university's chapel, which was quite liberal and inclusive. It was connected with justice issues and gave me a spiritual and social outlet.

Since you are now an active evangelical, I'm wondering how you weathered all these new challenges to the Bible's authority and the attempts to debunk the Judeo-Christian heritage.

Well, I did have a couple of high-school and junior-high teachers who had pushed me to look at things critically, so I had some preparation. In junior high I had read Lillian Hellman's memoir *Pentimento,* which is still one of my favorite books. We read it in a college English class, and the teacher tore it apart. That was hard at first, but then I began to see that you could be intensely critical with a text and still respect the text's integrity. After picking *Pentimento* to pieces, I still liked it and respected it. That helped me to see that you could be critical with the Bible and it would still hold up. You don't have to handle the Bible like it's made of eggshells.

So with all my questions, problems and doubts, I knew I didn't have to just throw the Bible out. I could look at it critically, and it would keep its integrity. But I had to be willing to accept that some of *my* views about it didn't hold up.

After graduation I still couldn't go back to my old church and feel comfortable, so I went to a liberal, socially active church near my home. I saw it as a good bridge between my Christian roots and my new interest in current events and social causes. I had become very interested in women's issues, and this church seemed to allow me to explore that while maintaining a connection to Christianity.

Then I went to graduate school in New York. I loved New York, but I hated graduate school. I had a scholarship and stipend on a Ph.D. track at an excellent university, but I knew within three weeks that I would finish my M.A. in a year and be gone. I had had enough of the academic life and all its inbred issues.

In New York I went to the Riverside Church because it had been an early supporter of Martin Luther King Jr. William Sloane Coffin had preached there during the civil rights movement, and they dealt with the social issues that were of concern to me. But I never met anyone there, so I didn't become a part of the church in any meaningful way.

After graduate school I got a job in New York and continued to meet lots of different people. I volunteered in an AIDS ward for babies. We would just go in and hold the babies and comfort them so that the medical staff could do the more technical jobs. Some of the women in that group were Jamaican, and they all seemed to come from *huge* families. I was the baby of my family, and they found it hysterical that this college girl didn't know how to change diapers. Those women were very far from my upper-middle-class suburban background, and I found a strength of character in them that made me look beyond the comfortable worldview of my old church.

At my job I worked closely with people who were gay, Jewish, agnostic and atheistic. My world was much bigger than it had been in my little church, and the questions kept getting broader, not narrower. In one way I wanted to set down my own spiritual roots, but I didn't want to have to stop thinking or caring to do it.

The biggest change came when I met the man who became my husband. He is a very hardline evangelical/fundamentalist who could tend, I suppose, to be a bit legalistic. But he was an echo from my past. We connected on a very deep level. Even though we would have raging arguments about abortion, women in the church—you name it—I respected his faith and his commitment to helping the poor.

We served together in Haiti. He worked in the hospital, and I was a teacher. That experience made me look even harder at what I believed. When we first got there, what I saw was like a physical metaphor for the human soul. I saw incredible physical privation. People who were sick would be carried miles—on a stretcher, on someone's back, even in a basket. They might or might not be seen by a doctor or nurse. I began to see the real nature of human existence when it's stripped of all its comfortable trappings.

The land in Haiti was overcrowded and worn out. People scraped by for the most basic hand-to-mouth existence. Farms, many which were just ragged little garden patches, covered the back yards, hills and shoulders of the roads. People scratched away at any piece of land that might grow a morsel of food. You would see a tiny little plot perched on a narrow ledge high up a steep cliff. There was a joke the Haitians told when someone would come to the clinic. You would ask how the patient was injured, and someone would say, "He fell out of his farm."

The land was almost gone. I remember thinking as we drove into the interior that it was like a lunar landscape. Just rocky hills with all the topsoil gone. The colonists started it by cutting down the hardwood forests, then the farmers cleared the land to grow food. Now they cut down what's left to make charcoal for cooking. The people are desperate, and they continue to use up what little nutrient value is left in the earth.

I can't really describe how frightening it was to see that. I had never fully understood how badly the earth could be abused, and with what horrible results. The population grows, and the land becomes less and less productive.

Once we hiked to an old fortress built in the nineteenth century to ward off Napoleon. This was shortly after the slave revolt that drove out the French. Nearby was the ruler's palace, built to resemble Versailles. It's all in ruins now, a symbol of a wanton lifestyle and a physical reminder of the huge chasm between the rich and poor.

That image really brought home the sinfulness of economic injustice. The fundamentalists had overlooked that part of the gospel, I felt, and that was more where my thinking was going at the time. I didn't see how all this emphasis on doctrine was worth much. I wondered if we really needed to go in there and take away the dignity that comes with an indigenous culture and its beliefs. Most of our group was white, and the Haitians are black. As an Asian-American I felt a bit like the interloper.

I remember meeting a missionary there who was vehemently opposed to bringing in any of the attributes of the voodoo gods as a way of explaining Christ. At that time some missionaries were reevaluating the ways they evangelized and trying to avoid complete destruction of the native culture. He seemed so combative and hard. I couldn't understand his narrowness, which at that time seemed very ethnocentric, maybe a bit racist. I'm still a bit uncomfortable with his tone, but I grew to understand his fundamentalist desire to completely separate Christianity from the paganism of voodoo.

The day in Haiti is defined by the sun. It starts at sunrise and ends at sundown. It gets very dark at night, and unless you have a generator, which almost no one has, you are a prisoner of the darkness until the sun comes up again. I saw that we really are just specks of dust in the universe, that our existence is very tenuous at best.

While we were there a big voodoo celebration was in progress. People would drink and dance and beat on drums all day long. At night they would travel around with big torches. It was not all benevolent. I could see how in that darkness people would make up stories to explain life and try to deal with its mysteries and dangers. It was a frightening time.

Aside from the eerie associations of drums and torches in the darkness, was there anything tangible to cause that sense of fear?

Yes. Things got out of control. Sometimes we would hear from the Haitians that a family had been singled out for retribution, and they would be completely defenseless against the mob. There was a well-grounded sense that life was completely unpredictable. People lived in constant fear—politically, spiritually and physically.

There was a violent coup in progress, and as foreigners we were quite vulnerable. Anger can be very arbitrary in that kind of a situation, and you can't depend on the structures that keep you safe at home. You can't just dial 911. In a society like that, where fear rules, everyone is just trying to keep out of harm's way. And gossip and rumor can turn deadly very fast.

You have talked about the political and physical fear. Can you give an example of spiritual fear?

Well, they are really all tied in together. Separating them out is somewhat arbitrary. But here's an example: my husband would see patients in the clinic, and when he would ask what their symptoms were, they would say, "Spirits are crawling in my blood." The physical and metaphysical were not separable to them.

Often they would have already gone to a voodoo healer, who would charge them an exploitative price—voodoo had an incredible power over people's lives.

I don't want to sound like I'm just denigrating Haiti. Haiti is an extreme example, a grotesque, of what can happen when fear and superstition rule people's lives. Some of the things we take for granted, like loving one's neighbors and being kind to others, are not givens in Haiti. They aren't necessarily the natural order of things. Not everyone has a sense of community or nation, where everyone is supposed to pull together for the common good.

I began to see why that missionary I mentioned before, and perhaps other Christians through the years, have taken a hard line against accommodating pagan beliefs. A lot of those pagan, or pre-Christian, belief systems were horribly racist, sexist and downright cruel. The Aztecs, for instance, had a virtual slaughterhouse to carry out their rituals.

It's still difficult to admit, because it grates on me to think exclusively, but the Judeo-Christian tradition has a lot going for it. Voodoo, like most pagan systems, is all based on appeasing angry, evil spirits. The Christian understanding of an all-powerful, loving God is not universal.

I began to really examine the idea of humbling myself before God. Then an old Southern preacher came by to lead a revival. He preached on the wheat and the tares, which was very appropriate for me at that moment because I had to decide whether I was going to submit to Christ or just stay on the fence.

I had to really examine the heart of the matter, as one of my high-school teachers used to say. I think that came from the Graham Greene novel *The Heart of the Matter.* The human heart can be very deceptive, but the heart of the matter is our sin and our need for redemption.

I struggled with the ramifications of subjecting my will to God, which I had not truly done before. I said, "God, I know you are true, but do I really have to die to myself to know you?" I had never really understood that part of the Word, but it was beginning to make sense.

After that I began to ease back into meditation on the Word, and I joined a Bible study group. My husband and I continued to argue and discuss things *(she laughs).*

After we were married we moved to the South and joined an evangelical church. Our pastor was African-American, and the congregation was a mixture of whites and blacks. He preached the Word, but there was also a holistic ministry that had been missing from my other evangelical experiences.

When you are a minority in this country, there is a sense that Christianity is a white religion. It makes you wonder if you really fit. That was a bit of an issue for me as an Asian-American. What I learned from my Southern pastor was that if he could go through all the racism and humiliation of being black in the South, especially back when he was young, and still emerge as a strong evangelical Christian, then maybe there was something transcendent that was bigger than race or culture.

In affluent, suburban-oriented churches the big issues seem to be family values and abortion. Those are real issues, but it always seemed to me that "family values" was code for looking out for ourselves in this ugly, scary world. Abortion is a contained issue. It's always expressed as Us versus Them. But there are other equally important issues that they don't want to acknowledge, because those problems would call for more than just protesting and making signs, and that's what made me search far and wide.

In our Southern church we dealt with all the global issues of peace, poverty and the environment. But lots of our friends, black and white, were concerned about abortion and family values. That made me reexamine my thinking and see the Christian experience in a much broader light. *She laughs.* I was surprised to find that some of my black friends were big-time Rush Limbaugh fans! I can't *stand* him myself! Sometimes my husband, who is white, listens to Limbaugh, and I just explode. "How can you stand him?" I yell. He says, "I just find it interesting to hear his perspective sometimes."

But in our Southern evangelical church I saw that issues and perspectives could transcend race, and that was very helpful. I thought only white people could like Rush Limbaugh!

I still get in some pretty heated debates with Christian friends who want to place others outside the fold. I think that's very dangerous thinking.

What kinds of people do they place outside the fold?

Well, often it's things related to sex: gay people, sexually active people, people who have had an abortion. We live in a fallen world, and people are going to sin. In the fundamentalist camp there's a sense of rating the sins.

I have friends who are gay, and when they have either been pushed out of Christian fellowship or chosen to leave, they have no standards to push them toward right decisions. My husband and I love each other very much, and we disagree on many, many important issues, but because we are Christians we can gauge our responses by the Bible and by what other Christians are saying. If you sever those ties, then you have to make up your own rules out of nothing.

So you would encourage homosexuals and unmarried people who are living together to be part of a worshiping community.

It's a difficult notion, but yes. If they are Christians I would trust the Holy Spirit to guide them. It's not as though those of us who are allowed or encouraged to stay in the church are without sin. We just sin in more acceptable ways.

I know this is a hard thing for people my parents' age, because they grew up with a very different way of thinking. My grandparents were very poor immigrant farmers. They and their kids faced poverty, racism and the fear of failing. My generation has the time to sit around and ponder these bigger questions, but I certainly don't see my generation as wiser or better. We have just been given a different situation to work from.

I have the greatest respect for my parents' generation. In my home church the older generation, whatever their faults, were very kind, generous, humble people. They were very oriented to service. I think of them as very sweet, warm people.

I don't know what happened to the younger people who came of age in the seventies and eighties, though. They hold outwardly to fundamentalist doctrine, but they're much more like yuppies in their values. I have a difficult time with that.

They put up polite barriers. They seem to be saying, "We have our friends, thank you." If you play tennis or basketball, or if you have put together an impressive stereo system, you can be in their clique. Oh, you also have to share their brand of humor. To sum up, there's an underdeveloped sense of how to bring in others. I never felt a part of that group.

My dad and the old guard get very frustrated when they are trying to train up new deacons and treasurers to take their places. There's a general reluctance of younger people to take responsibility. It's the family values thing again. "First we have to make sure our unit is intact, *then* maybe we can do something."

The old folks don't understand, because they had families too when they founded that church. Big families in many cases. They worked harder, for less money, but they never questioned their responsibility to serve. That individualistic, family values notion is like quicksand.

Now that you have moved from the Deep South to the more cosmopolitan South, what is your church experience?

It's very monocultural. They have a strong sense of foreign missions but a general reluctance to get involved with the world around us. It's a family values thing, I guess. Very homogeneous.

Down in the Deep South there was a vibrancy. The whites thought the church service was too black. Too noisy. The blacks thought it was too white and reserved. As an Asian I don't know where I fit, but our bond was in Christ, and working through those issues was what made it such a halcyon experience.

Because that church was so open to its own diversity, I could bring people to it. I had a friend down there from college who was still a lefty humanist, but she came to church with me because it was so compelling. She sensed the power and love. I miss that, and I don't know if I'll ever get to experience it again.

But who knows? Ten years ago I would never have imagined myself married and living in the Deep South, let alone going to a conservative church where black people listened to Rush Limbaugh! And I didn't really expect to feel a sense of God's power. When I got there I was surprised. Maybe I'll be surprised again.

Part 3

Sexuality: From Abuse to Ecstasy

13

The Girl in the Basement

She's a professional in her late thirties, a mother of young children and active in a parachurch ministry to teenagers. We meet at a park on a sunny weekday afternoon and sit on a bench watching her young sons, who have recently learned to swim.

The park is relatively uncrowded; the lifeguard has only a dozen or so kids to watch. Her boys swim with joyful abandon, jumping off the dock, sliding down the fiberglass slide and diving for coins in the cool lake water. They remain in the water for several hours, seeming to be some aquatic hybrid: part seal, part human.

She's a quiet woman with dark, deeply communicative eyes and an unassuming but very engaging smile. As we speak, I find that although she is reserved, she is not shy. She speaks forcefully, though kindly. I get the impression that she would not be a pushover for anyone.

When I first met her I had expected her to be reticent, but she is quite comfortable talking about the repeated sexual abuse that shaped her childhood spirituality and later her adult response to God.

She grew up in a very conservative church and attended a fundamentalist college in another part of the country. Her older siblings parted company with the family church over issues related to the Vietnam War and the social upheaval of the sixties. Her parents left the church later, mainly because of the unkind response to their children's questioning.

* * *

Even though I am now in my forties, it's not easy for me to say that I was sexually abused. I now know that I shouldn't feel guilty about being abused by my uncle from age four to eight, as though it were my fault, but the old feelings don't die quickly. Years of suppressing what occurred and how I felt about it have not helped.

Also, when I and others first went public with our stories of abuse, society and, I'm sad to say, often Christians were quick to see Christian male abusers as men who were caught at a weak moment, who needed to be rescued from their lapse of control, comforted and protected from the consequences of their stumble into sin. This reaction of considering the abuser to be the real victim has only added to the confusion of those of us who have been abused.

I wish that I could say that growing up in the church was a healing process for me. I hope my story is different from others', but I feel that my confusion and pain were only intensified by the church.

Growing up in the fifties and sixties, it seemed as if the main focus of sexual guidance was to teach sexual restraint for the purpose of protecting girls' virginity. This would ensure their "niceness," their marriageability and their right to have happy Christian homes. Not being sexually innocent and untouched, I was convinced from a very early age that I was not nice, would never date or marry, and would never reach the esteemed image of a Christian wife and mother. I never felt close to other girls, because I couldn't join in their hours of girlish chatter about their first kiss, their boyfriend or their dreams of being a bride in white. I knew that I was damaged goods. I was somehow different and nongirlish throughout my teenage years. I felt asexual.

My heart would cringe when we were instructed on the importance of being kind, obedient girls. I felt guilty that I had not told my parents during or after the years when my uncle would ask me to go to the basement with him while they visited upstairs with my aunt.

How did he explain the fact that he was disappearing into the basement with a little girl while the other adults visited?

Everyone knew I was his favorite. He had all sorts of hobbies, and he would use the pretext that we were going to go look at his latest projects. I disliked being alone with him, yet I was told how lucky I was to be his favorite niece who he always sought out. I felt uneasy with him, but he was kind in a strange sort of way. He brought me nice presents on my birthdays, and I was aware that he thought I was special. I could feel his warm looks at me, singling me out in a room. I felt guilty for not being appreciative.

In Sunday school we were always taught that it was not godly to trust your natural emotions, that instead of pleasing ourselves we should please others, that we should not hurt other people's feelings, and that we should always obey—never say to an adult, "No, I don't want to."

I felt I was being unloving and unkind when I did not respond affectionately to my uncle's obvious pleasure in me. I felt as though it was I who was bad and had caused the problem.

I suppose at that young age you hadn't been taught specifics of sexuality—what was right and wrong, where the limits were and when you had the right to say no?

No, we were pretty much in the dark, even in our later school years. But my uncle never physically forced me to do anything, and he never spoke to me harshly. He only asked me to do things that made me feel uncomfortable—and relieved that the basement was so dark. With his calm, gentle and eager voice I felt that his feelings were the reasonable ones and that I could not deny him. I childishly reasoned, How could a nice girl say, "No, I don't like your attentiveness," "No, I don't feel comfortable sitting on your lap," "No, I don't want to go into the basement with you," "No, I don't want you to do that," when he always seemed so kind? Even though I did not enjoy being around him at all, I knew my presence gave him great enjoyment.

So for four confusing years the trips to the basement continued. My simple concepts of sin and obedience grew entangled. I knew I should never lie, and so when he regularly made me promise never to tell anyone our secret, I never considered breaking my word and becoming guilty of telling a lie. Even when he detained me from going back upstairs until I had promised to be his special girl even when I had grown ladies' breasts, I felt I was bound before God to continue in this increasingly unpleasant relationship.

You seem to be saying that you knew something was wrong with him, even though you felt bound before God not to tell. At what age were you able to see clearly that he was wrong and that you were not to blame?

I know that my reexamination of the religious instruction I received as a child has been much of the core of my healing as an adult, but as a child bound by honor to keep silent, I was left to glean the spiritual truths on my own. From the church I constantly heard that "all have sinned and fallen short of God's glory." I felt that I was chief among all sinners and that I was fated to continue in that state because I believed I had voluntarily participated, even though I hated the experience.

Did you come to hate your uncle?

No, although when he died a few years later I felt glad—or, I should say, relieved that he was gone and that I didn't have to see him or deal with him anymore. But then I felt terribly guilty about that, and about the fact that everyone noticed that I shed no tears for the uncle who supposedly loved me and called me his favorite. I tried to muster up tears because he had died without Christ, but I couldn't feel sorrow at his passing—only more self-loathing.

How did all this spiritual confusion affect the way you reacted to the gospel message in church and Sunday school?

I eagerly accepted the truth that God's love and forgiveness embraced all those who came openly to the cross. I even used recess time at school to teach other children about God's love and his Word. I longed to share with others God's freedom and promise of an abundant life, because I felt that I could not participate in that joy. How could

I, being bad and having so many secrets, come openly to the cross?

Looking back, I now know that people saw me as a beautiful, quiet child. Because I grew up in a circle of family and friends, I was often praised for being such a nice Christian girl. But instead of those words soothing my guilt, they only added to my feelings of condemnation in that I could not dare to contradict their words or reveal my bad secrets. And so I would avoid their praise by looking down—only to be thought all the nicer for my modesty.

I was accepted and held up as a sensible young lady, but I actually felt like I was unfeminine and asexual. I was considered quiet, shy and serious when I was actually lost in morbid thoughts of self-hatred. People thought that I was lucky to be loved in a good Christian family, yet I felt that no one loved *me,* because they did not know the girl in the basement. I was seen as an obedient Christian girl, yet I did not make conscious choices. I just didn't know that I could ever say no.

But in God's grace, the sexual abuse did stop when I was eight. Although I still don't remember it, my mother recently told me that I had innocently asked her what a certain two-handed gesture meant. When she wanted to know why I had asked, I told her that my uncle had shown me the gesture. She and my father grew suspicious and ended the visits to my uncle and aunt's house. My mother even called the parents of my girl cousins to warn them of my uncle's problems, but sadly, they didn't believe her.

Did she know back then that he had actually been molesting you?

No. She assumed that she had stopped a bad situation before it had happened, and she never discussed my abusive uncle with me until I was in my late thirties. Actually, I thought she didn't know about my uncle, and all these years I kept from telling her because of a mixture of my own shame and a desire to save her and my dad the grief. Also, I like my aunt, and since my uncle has been dead all these years it seemed pointless to bring it up.

Then, amazingly, my mother told me that she had been sexually abused by her stepfather from age eight to thirteen. That opened the doors for her and me to share openly, for the first time, our long-held secrets.

Your experience, while tragic, is not unlike that of many girls who aren't raised in Christian families. Without mitigating your experience, it sounds like your faith ultimately pulled you through.

My faith in Christ is what made the difference, but the church, which is a different thing altogether, was less than helpful. The teaching about sex was so based on staying a virgin that they didn't seem to realize that not every girl gets to make that choice. Because I felt like damaged goods, I felt that nothing the church taught had anything to do with me personally. As I became a young woman I was left with a lot of confusing baggage.

Can you talk about that?

I didn't really date much in high school. If a boy showed any interest in me, I ran the other way. My husband says that when he asked me out in our senior year, I just said, "I'll have to ask my mom," and kept walking. He was persistent and kept after me, but when we would get close I would start to bail out emotionally.

After my experience with my uncle I felt that I just couldn't marry, because sex was such a distasteful idea. I did have sexual feelings. But my sexual feelings just made me feel guilty, and I didn't know how to deal with them.

The bigger issue was my basic faith in Christ. As I said, people assumed that I was a nice, obedient Christian teenager, when really I was full of self-loathing and doubt. I went to a very fundamentalist college, mainly to test once and for all whether there was anything to Christianity or whether I should just dump the whole thing.

How did that work out for you?

Well, in some ways it could have been the end. I saw how much the gospel could be tainted by culture, especially in fundamentalist and evangelical circles. The right-wing politics, the racism and the stress on outward appearances just about did me in. I had some pretty rocky times after I left home, but my faith in Christ—not the church—is stronger now. I have seen that Christ forgives us and calls us to him, regardless of what we have done or where we have been.

My husband went through a similar time, but we are both active Christians today. As far as church goes, we long for a worship

y active in church. We don't
s and politics of church life,
urch, we just attend Sunday-

was a big issue for the first
often or with such devastat-
—he's not terribly quick to
very confused by my confu-
able to accept a compliment
ld me I looked pretty, I would
at I was mocking him.

We have always had a pretty active sex life, and I enjoyed it. But after we were intimate, the next day I would feel violated and need space from him. He would take my emotional distance as a personal rejection. Then I would feel rejected by his lack of understanding. It was very hard to overcome. The church didn't have anything much to offer for dealing with those kinds of issues, which were at the core of our marriage.

How did you overcome the confusion about sex?

My husband studied the effects of sexual abuse before there was a lot of literature on it. He even called one of his old college psychology professors. It was pretty hit-and-miss, but he wanted to understand. He read about Jeffrey Masson and the reevaluation of Freud's rape myth theories, and we would talk about all of that.

Then, after all those years of suffering in isolation, seeing professionals stand up for victims and getting the support of family and friends has helped to muffle the despair of silence. The whole issue is treated differently today.

When I was a little girl, society at large was not exactly up to speed in helping children who were victims of sexual abuse, but given the thrust of the gospel, you would think that the church would have taken the lead. The church didn't really want to see the ramifications of sexual abuse, though.

A few years ago this was evident to me in a situation where an influential member of our church was sexually abusing a teenager in the congregation. The girl told me about it, so my husband and I had to confront the man. The deacon board's response was that the girl had initiated it, and they stood by the man. That was pretty typical of Christian thinking on the subject until very recently.

I could understand that to the deacons it might look like this girl had seduced an influential Christian leader. So, with the strength of prayer, I tried to help them understand. When I tried to explain the dynamics of sexual abuse and manipulation to them, I told them that I understood because I had been abused as a child. Their response was, "Maybe you're too close to this situation and you shouldn't be involved." It was like I was still damaged goods. They never did get it. The man moved on, and they covered up for him when he got a job in another church. My husband called that church and told the pastor, which is what our deacons had promised to do but didn't.

Is that partly why you aren't as active in church as you might otherwise be?

It's the kind of experience that makes me see the weaknesses of the church. They were just wrong. I don't think that I would be so stonewalled if it happened to one of the teenagers I work with now. That specific issue of sexual abuse is being handled much better, but when I see the mean-spirited and insensitive ways that so many Christians approach the issues of abortion and homosexuality, I see the same arrogance and lack of Christlike love. Again, too many people are charging in and making great pronouncements without thinking about the people God loves and died for: all sinners.

The self-assured leaders of the fundamentalist church of my youth weren't able to know the girl in the basement, let alone minister to her, because the worldview they had set up didn't have room for them to think the way they would have to think in order to know her. What about the Christians, or at least the kids raised in churches, who are homosexual or who have had an abortion? What are they hearing in all the shouting and condemning?

Christ's love is bigger and deeper than any issue. I'm more interested in loving Jesus and loving my neighbor than in espousing a pro or con statement on issues. Christ's call of love and grace to us isn't aimed at groups—it's aimed at all individuals who have needs.

She gestures, smiling, at her boys as they splash toward the ladder and climb up onto the dock. They take a running leap into the water, disappear and then surface, rolling onto their backs and spouting like little whales. Do you see the joy and peace those boys are feeling right now? I hope to raise those two little swimmers to feel the same joy and peace in their relationship with Christ.

14

I Left My Tribe When I Came Out as a Lesbian

She's a leader in the lesbian community of a large city who has written articles and led workshops on the subject of fundamentalism and the lesbian experience. I wonder if she will be somewhat hostile when I call, but a mutual friend has assured her that I'm on the level and won't misuse her words. She's articulate, friendly and very concerned that her comments not be used to put down fundamentalist Christians like her parents, with whom she has a somewhat tentative relationship.

Twice after the interview she calls me back to clarify statements that she fears might seem unkind or judgmental. We talk again, going over issues that could be hurtful to lesbians or fundamentalists. She restates her points and asks me to read back what she has said. She wants to be sure that I got it right.

* * *

I decided to start a support group for lesbian ex-fundamentalists just to have some company. I had left the church in my twenties and came out as a lesbian about five years later. I had a friend who had been raised fundamentalist, and every time we talked these issues kept coming up. I had been in a twelve-step program, and I just adapted it to the issues facing ex-fundamentalist lesbians.

It was an interesting group of women. Most of us had been leaders in the church—youth directors, choir members, you name it. I wondered why there weren't a lot of people who had just sat in the pews, and I think I now know. The movers and shakers, the ones who are creative and energetic, are the ones who have the courage and strength to get out. Many others just stay in their churches.

It was hard to leave. I left my tribe. As a fundamentalist I had a lifestyle, complete with its own language, dress and behavior that made me part of the inner circle.

In the ex-fundamentalist support group we found ourselves using lines like "I have a burden . . ." that we hadn't used for years. As fundamentalists we had felt ourselves part of the chosen, the select who were going to heaven when Jesus came back for us. It's hard to leave that mindset.

Being a fundamentalist was always work. Even as a kid. You could play with the unsaved, but you always had to witness to them. At school you had to be a testimony at all times and try to turn every encounter, every discussion, into a witnessing opportunity. It made you stand out.

It's hard enough being a teenager! Especially for a girl, and particularly a lesbian. It's so difficult to find a sense of self, and then when you are constantly told to be selfless, it is even more difficult.

There may be some fundamentalist women who have a strong, functional sense of self, but I haven't met one yet. You're always on guard duty, looking for heresy, backsliding or slip-ups. I have a lot of issues with my family that keep me from feeling like I belong there. Maybe in my next life I'll have a sense of family.

You get a sense of belonging in youth group. Anyone is "accepted" into a youth group because they are proof that the group is working. You're a potential convert, member or leader. So even if they can't stand you, they accept you. You get to be in the holy huddle, and after a while it seems like you're accepted into a kind of family, but there are a lot of strings attached.

I used to hear so many stories about people who left the church. They had gone over the hill, so to speak, into that unknown land called "the world." The idea of actually leaving filled me with fear. I was so sheltered that I found it very difficult to be out in the world. The first time I went into a bar (and I don't generally frequent bars, by the way) I was *so* apprehensive. I asked the bartender, "Do you serve food in here?" and was immediately carded *(she laughs).*

When I came out I discarded all my spiritual identity, and I had nothing to replace it with. As a lesbian I simply could not be in the church in any way. I felt this incredible void. I had no idea how to relate to God except in the ways I had been taught. So I had nothing.

A lot of gay women, and a lot of women in general, are drawn to the Greek idea of the goddess, perhaps because they have been completely shut out of their fundamentalist heritage. There are groups like Gays for Jesus that still preach Jesus as Savior and Lord, but I found that I couldn't be a part of that. I find spiritual solace more in Buddhist teachings now. I meet with a Buddhist priest for whom my lesbianism is not a barrier, so I can pursue spiritual things again.

Looking back, I would have to say that the friends I had in the church weren't really friends. I made my first real friends in my twenties, after I had left.

I went back to a wedding at my home church. That was a real eye-opener. I must have been so *dull* as a teenager! People came up to me and said, "What happened to you?" Later I looked at pictures of myself, and I really looked boring. In the support group we all brought pictures of ourselves from our teenage fundamentalist days. One woman, who now has a hairstyle you might call a crew cut, showed a picture of herself in a nice little dress, with a very fundamentalist hair style. Big hair! Beehive! It was hilarious! Those pictures seemed like they were of other people.

I see myself as a recovering fundamentalist because for me it was an obsessive behavior. We called our lesbian ex-fundamentalist support group a *no-step* program. Many of us had been in other twelve-step programs, and we didn't want this to be *more* work. We wanted to just share our—I almost said burdens—common experiences and try to get free from some similar baggage.

I still think in very right-and-wrong terms. My friends always tell me, "You have more than two choices." Most things are more complex than simply right and wrong, but that's the way I was taught, and it stays with you: One way is right. It's God's way. Anything else is simply wrong. Period.

As a kid, I remember hearing people at testimony time say, "God spoke to me." I wondered if they meant out loud, like an audible voice. I wondered if I should be literally hearing God's voice, and if I was bad for not hearing it—as if I was less holy.

In some ways my sexual orientation, which I didn't understand back then, was almost a positive. You weren't exactly encouraged to get into heavy petting with boys, so my lack of sexual experimentation was seen by the church people as a sign of piety. I became something of a role model because I fit the image of a pious girl who was saving herself for marriage. It wasn't manipulative on my part; I just accepted what people said about me. I wasn't at all drawn to boys, and I believed that it was a result of my spiritual commitment. Later on I began to suspect that there might be another reason.

Did you leave the church specifically because of your sexual orientation?

No. I left the church out of sheer boredom. I just knew that there was a bigger life out there. I gradually came to terms with being a lesbian. It was not an abrupt awareness or a driving force that was pushing me out of the church. I certainly didn't know that I was a lesbian when I was in the church.

Now I am the only one in my family who is not a fundamentalist, and I don't see them very often. There are a lot of issues that keep us from having any real time together.

I remember the first time my parents witnessed to me after I came out as a lesbian. I knew all the lines, all the angles, because I had used them all myself, so it was like listening to a record. I don't mean that in a nasty way, but it wasn't a discussion, it was a witnessing opportunity. The witnessing keeps happening whenever we're together. We can't have a real talk, because they have to maneuver me into a place where they can witness. I say, "Mom, you're witnessing again!"

But of course she is. She has to. Her job with me is not done unless all of her kids are in the fold. I know it has to be hard for her to tell people about me. I'm sure I'm the subject of several prayer groups. I'm an ugly mark on my mom and dad's record as Christian parents.

Have they tried to understand your perspective? Are they open to reading about lesbianism?

I tried to give my father something to read, but he just said, "I've read everything I need to read." Once he asked me, when I was home on a visit, "Do you people colonize?" I guess he wanted to know if I was going to try to convert or seduce other people. I said no, and he's never brought it up again.

Although we can't talk at all, my folks have made some gestures that were nice. My mother bought tickets for us to attend a concert performed by our city's women's chorus, which has a lot of lesbians in it. She can't say the L-word, but it was her way of letting me know that on some level she accepted me as a person.

Looking back, do you see your acceptance of Christ as a sham, or was it genuine?

I grew up feeling that I really loved Jesus, but it seemed that I could never do enough to earn his love. I saw a lot of terrible spiritual and psychic damage done in the name of loving Jesus. For instance, there was a preacher in our area who pastored three churches. When his teenage daughter got pregnant she had to go before each one of those congregations and confess her sin. All three! Now for whose benefit was that? Her dad's. Not hers, that's for sure. Why did all those people let that happen? Why didn't someone in one of those congregations put a stop to that humiliating experience? Why didn't anyone think of the girl's needs?

So now I have to say that I look more at actions than words. I tried to explain that to my mother—that I can see good, as well as evil, in a lot of people. But she can't see any good without the cross. Anything kind or just or compassionate done by a Buddhist, for instance, counts as nothing for her. She told me that I had a tissue-paper faith.

There is a keen sense of warfare in the fundamentalist church. When you go to school you're "behind enemy lines." Your teachers, your classmates, are all potential enemies, and you have to be on guard all the time. I could never go back to that.

15

God Loves Me More Than He Loves His Own Rules

We meet for coffee near the supermarket where she has worked for several years. She's a short, compact woman with the strong bearing of someone who spends her days in demanding physical labor.

We have talked on the telephone twice, and she has agreed to meet with me to talk about a subject that she feels is rarely dealt with honestly in the church: sex. This was particularly true, she says, of the fundamentalist church in which she was raised.

But she's no Dr. Ruth. Her interest is not clinical, but personal. Too many of her friends' marriages are sinking, and she feels strongly that their shared Christian background was more of a hindrance than a help.

Married for many years, she's the mother of two teenagers and is somewhat active in an evangelical church. As a child she attended a fundamentalist church and is still acquainted with several women she grew up with in youth activities. She says she is not a joiner and prefers a few close relationships to many shallow ones.

It's raining outside, and the wind is blowing fat droplets against the window where we sit. The coffee shop is fairly quiet as we pick up our conversation where it ended on the telephone.

* * *

As an adult I began to see that many of my friends had big sexual hang-ups that often played a part in the breakup of their marriages. I remember sitting in a Bible study with some other women when I was in my early thirties and just beginning to get reinvolved in Christian activities. One woman had a very abusive husband, and she had gotten the idea, from a Christian seminar, that she should endure it. She had taken the whole "submit to your husband" teaching very literally, so she would have sex on demand with this guy who hit her and wouldn't let her get a driver's license.

Then, here's the part that makes me want to scream: a local Christian counselor told her to kneel and assume the position of Christ in Gethsemane while her husband beat her. This was supposed to increase her knowledge of Christ and be a witness to her husband.

I take it this counselor was a man?

She looks at me like I'm the village idiot. Yes, as a matter of fact, he was a man—now that you mention it. *She grins, wondering if I get the sarcasm.*

I know, dumb question. Sorry. Please continue.

I can't imagine a female counselor coming up with a crazy S&M fantasy like that, can you? The non-Christian husband and those conservative Christian counselors shared a common view of a woman's place. That literalist interpretation of Scripture has more to do with abusing women than with following Christ.

I spent a lot of years overcoming the legacy of my childhood sexual abuse, and I have no patience at all with such woman-hating advice or the people who dish it out. I told her to pack her bags, call a cab and head for Mama's, but I didn't know her very well, and she didn't see me as someone worth listening to.

Any ideas why she would feel that way? It would seem that your advice would be a breath of fresh air.

As a sexually abused kid, I grew up feeling kind of sexless, and that's still the way a lot of women see me. I'm not in the game as far as they are concerned. I don't spend the time on diets, tanning, cosmetics and all that other stuff. I probably seem like a frumpy old housewife to them, and their sexual appeal is a big part of who they are. But a lot of those women are horribly dysfunctional. They are thinking of sex as something you obediently permit. It is part of submitting to your husband. It's really screwed up. You get all dolled up to catch a man, then you have to please him even if you can't stand him. Then you can't figure out why he doesn't respect you as a person.

I hate to think of the kinds of authoritative fathers and brothers they must have grown up with. I can't imagine my father or brothers telling me to let a man beat me. Their example taught me the way it should be. When my father found out about the relative who was sexually abusing me, he never blamed me or saw me as anything other than a victim.

We were always taught that the Catholic Church (that whore of Babylon) was apostate because they considered the pope to be infallible. But fundamentalists have their popes too. Back then Bill Gothard's word was revered like it came from the apostle Paul or a prophet. Same with Hal Lindsey. Now it's Dr. Dobson. Those guys had a few good ideas, but then they got elevated to the level of a pope. Their pronouncements are like Scripture to some fundamentalists. Try criticizing anything one of them says. You'll probably get hate mail if you print this.

Once I was in a fellowship with some fairly close female friends, and we got on the topic of sex. Everybody wanted to know . . . *She pauses and grins, looking a bit surprised at where this conversation has gone.* Am I way off the track here? I'm comfortable with this, but I don't want to waste your time if this isn't what you're interested in.

Actually, I think that this will be very helpful to some readers. I don't want to pry into your life, though. Please continue only if you feel comfortable.

Okay. I wish I could have read something like this a few years back when I was working this all out in relative isolation.

There is a pretty big silence about specifics of sexuality in conservative churches. Everyone in the group wanted to know what was "normal"—positions, oral sex, stuff like that. This was in the seventies, when society was starting to talk about female orgasms and other previously unmentionable topics.

One woman wanted to know if it was sinful to let your husband tie you up. Not in a mean way, but to heighten pleasure. She had read about it in a women's magazine article, and it had obviously piqued her interest. She really wanted to know what we all thought, but everyone just sat there clinching their coffee cups until someone made a silly remark, and then she quickly acted like she had only been joking.

Growing up in fundamentalist churches, you get the idea that sex should be the missionary position in the dark once a week. I knew that my friends really wanted to know what other Christians did in bed as a way of examining their own attitudes. Television shows and magazine articles gave them all these ideas, but they couldn't talk about them without pretending to be disgusted.

Some people would question why we need to discuss exotic or unusual sexual activities.

I know. But people aren't unaware of the social issues around them. Look at all the divorces you see now in fundamentalist and evangelical circles. If people are reading about sexual experimentation, and especially female sexual satisfaction, then they are going to get tired of the old missionary position. They will figure that they can be Christians or they can have fun in bed. That's what happened to some of the people I knew.

When I got married, I had to examine all my confused feelings about sex, starting from the basics, because the sexual abuse had messed me up so much. So I could have added a lot to that discussion, but I also knew that if I opened up to them, the details of my sex life would be all over the town. I had already heard details about other people's sex lives from those women. I don't mind talking about sex if it will be helpful, but not so that people can live vicariously through my sex life. So I just kept quiet. Besides, I was new to the group, and

I didn't want to get labeled as some kind of hippie sex maniac.

Having been sexually abused as a girl, I had two choices. I could live a life of sexual repression, or I could get to work and try to figure things out. I lived a very repressed life as a girl, but when I fell in love and married, I had to work through my sexual feelings or see my marriage shrivel up and die. Besides, my sexual self had been stolen from me and I wanted it back. Now I think I'm a lot less hung up about sex than my Christian friends who dated through high school and did all the girl things.

What do you mean by "girl things"?

Pajama parties, Barbie dolls, doing your hair and nails. I hated all that stuff, and I still do. I tried to disappear sexually, to not flaunt it or act it out even in the most mundane way. In church we got all this antisex talk, but the subculture was as sexually charged as anywhere, and it was heavily oriented toward manipulation. All the coyness, stuffing tissue into your bra, flirting and teasing—I still hate that stuff.

I'm not saying that my husband and I haven't had our problems, but we have always had a pretty passionate relationship, and we have spent a lot of time working through our feelings of guilt.

Guilt about what?

Well, like a lot of people, we were having sex before we were married. But we pretended that we weren't. I understand the ideal of chastity, and I believe in it, but you don't teach that to kids by telling them all kinds of fairy tales about sex. The end result of our fundamentalist upbringing was that we saw sex as dirty. Having been sexually abused just added to that. So we would have sex and then feel terrible about it. Every now and then someone I knew would get pregnant, and the way they were viewed at church would confirm our guilty feelings.

Some of my friends seem schizophrenic about sex. They dress up a lot more seductively than me. For example, look at my sensible haircut. I don't go out wearing dresses with cleavage. I don't plan to buy the Wonderbra. I hate high heels. I don't wear clingy pants or blouses. I wear modest bathing suits in public. So I probably seem a bit prudish. But actually I have felt okay about moonlight swimming in the nude or sunbathing topless if we're just with a couple of really close friends at a private beach. *She stops and studies my response, then laughs nervously.* I'm unloading on you, aren't I?

You are what we call a cooperative interview subject. (We both laugh.) *I think that this will be helpful, though. So if you feel okay, please continue.*

Some of my friends, the ones who wear the high-cut bathing suits and low-cut dresses, were actually experiencing some pretty severe sexual dysfunction in their marriages. Meanwhile, dowdy little me was having great sex with the man I loved. I wish now that I could have just spoken freely with them, because they were acting like they were these sexually hot numbers, but actually they were having infrequent, dissatisfying sex (or no sex) with their husbands. They were the ones who really wanted to ask questions, but they couldn't share honestly, so they blabbed about other people's sex lives. I think they were desperately trying to make sense out of their confusion, but all that vague talk about submitting to their husbands wasn't helping. They dressed and flirted like they were sexually liberated, but then they didn't like where it led.

Those mixed signals helped lead to divorces for some of them. One guy in particular really resented his flirty wife's sexy dressing. They rarely had sex, and when they did she hated it. He got more and more angry and finally found sex elsewhere. But where were they going to be able to talk about those issues without having their private business served up as food for the gossip banquet?

I wish we could have talked honestly—really honestly—without having it become like a tabloid newspaper. The fundamentalist legacy got rolled over by the so-called sexual revolution. We were raised to think of sex as bad and dirty outside of marriage and something you didn't discuss *in* marriage. Then we were hit by a sexually obsessed culture and had to act like we had the abundant life in all areas since we were Christians. It's dangerous to start from the position that you already have a better life than unbelievers in every area. You can't grow. You can't even ask questions. I don't see where the Bible tells us we will have all the answers to life as soon as we believe in Christ.

A friend of mine from church died of AIDS recently, and I think I learned more about Christ's love from him than I have from any preacher or book. Every time I was with him since I found out about his infection, I was just driven to my knees before the Lord.

He, like me, was a good Christian young person. He went to youth group; he obeyed his parents and tried very hard to be a good witness. But he had never felt attracted to girls. Only to boys. His first homosexual experience just sort of happened with another boy from church. I didn't know that boy very well, because he left and became openly gay once the rumors started. I have no idea where he is now.

Don, my friend, did everything to hide his homosexuality well into his thirties. We would always wonder why he wasn't married, since many girls, myself included, had crushes on him.

But he led a secret life of promiscuous sex that increased his self-hatred. He couldn't accept the idea that he might be one of those hated "faggots" that people snickered about, so he tried to be the model of a conservative Christian man. I have a gay colleague, by the way, who fears two groups: skinheads and Christians. To her, they act and sound the same.

Can you explain that? The skinheads have a pretty different agenda from the fundamentalists, don't they?

Maybe from our point of view, but from her position it all sounds the same. When you feel persecuted (and remember that it wasn't too long ago that homosexuals were being locked up in mental wards and being given electroshock therapy or even lobotomies), anyone who yells at you and calls you names is pretty scary. Being told you're going to burn in hell doesn't sound much different from being told you are going to die in the gas chambers. The old "hate the sin but love the sinner" rings pretty hollow when you're being screamed at and threatened.

But Don got past all of that. After he got sick he was forced to accept himself for who he was, and then he finally learned that God loved him unconditionally. He wasn't clear on what to do about his sexual orientation. He went into an ex-gay ministry for a while and tried living as a celibate homosexual. Then he would go through periods where he would just give in and be with guys. But he knew that he couldn't earn God's love any more than he could lose it, and that freed him to really examine his own life and his relationship with God.

He had a serious sexual addiction, and he told me when he was in his thirties that he was trying to establish the sense of sexual self that heterosexuals get to work on openly from puberty through adulthood. He had been in the closet his whole adult life, and now he had to do twenty years of self-examination in the few years he had left. But he was one of the holiest men I have ever known.

The man you have just described won't come across in print as a holy man to a lot of Christians. Can you explain what you mean by "holy"?

Don knew that he was a sinner. He had known that since his first sexual encounter. I mean, how could he not know that, growing up as a fundamentalist? But he was starting to realize that he was no more a sinner than anyone else. He came from a psychologically abusive home, so we would talk about our backgrounds and how they would affect our sexual selves.

I could be honest with him in a way that I couldn't with other Christians who were trying to keep up the façade of holiness. After Don let everyone in the church know that he had contracted AIDS from a life of multiple homosexual partners, there was little left to speculate about. He said, "Let them gossip." They did anyway, but he was beyond trying to pull the wool over people's eyes.

I found that I could talk to him about my background. I was like a lot of girls who have been sexually abused. I was never flirtatious in my actions or dress, and I deflected any sexual overtures, no matter how innocent. I still have trouble accepting a compliment from my husband. But after all those years of denying my sexuality, I became very sexual with my boyfriend. I was in love, and I had distanced myself from church since I had never felt that I fit in with the nice, pure girls. While dating, I had all these powerful feelings and a need to be passionately loved. So I went from total repression to a serious lack of restraint. But they were both the result of denial and a lack of understanding. If I had dated in high school, I probably would have been pregnant by tenth grade. Now when I see kids, or even adults, get into sexual trouble, I can understand that it's not sex that is the problem. Sex is a way we express our innermost selves, and if we are spiritually hurt, our sexual lives will be broken.

Neither Don nor I was "worse" than the other. His brokenness just gave him a deadly virus. Neither of us was "bad" in that we wanted to sin or rebel. We were hurt, confused people, and that was acted out sexually.

We talked about the way our fundamentalist background, with all its rules and its fear of gossip, missed our emotional selves. He helped me to understand the tyranny of church gossip—how it forces everyone to deny their sinfulness and deep need for a Savior. I began to understand why we can't accept our own sin or the sin of others, and how that keeps us from being honest. We had both lived lives of covering up, hiding and hating ourselves. We both had to start being honest with ourselves when we got into sexual trouble.

Once Don, my husband and I stayed up late into the night talking about the majesty of God's grace. Don wasn't sick then, but he had some AIDS-related illnesses, and he knew that he quite likely wouldn't live beyond his thirties or forties. That freed him, in a sense, to drop all pretenses. I can't really describe that night, but it was the most liberating, humbling experience I have known. I knew that God loved me more than he loved his own rules, or the rules that get tacked on by churches trying to be extra holy.

When Don died, my girlfriend called around to let some of the church families know. She was in tears after that, and she's still hurt and angry two years later. One woman who had known Don from infancy asked very judgmentally, "What did he expect?" Another lifelong acquaintance coolly pronounced, without grief: "I don't see how anyone can read the Bible and do *that.*"

Before reconnecting with Don I probably would have called those women up and yelled at them, but Don showed me that judgmental, condemning Christians who gossip are just messed up like we all are. Like us, they can tolerate their own sins but not those of others. I feel truly sorry for those women, because they have all driven at least some of their own kids away with their judgmental, mean spirit . . . See, there I go judging them *(she laughs).* I can't stand that kind of behavior any more than they can stand the idea of a Christian who has gotten pregnant out of wedlock or led a homosexual lifestyle. *She smiles warmly with a hint of embarrassment, but the embarrassment fades quickly. She takes a sip of her coffee and ponders her thoughts for a moment.*

I try to remember to pray for those women. My husband is better with words than I am in these situations, and he's planning to write a letter to each one. Not to scold them, but to give them brotherly encouragement to call my girlfriend and apologize. My girlfriend is stumbling in her faith, and I don't believe that, deep in their hearts, they want to drive her away from Christ. That's what they have done, though. My girlfriend has lots of unbelieving friends who would never treat her that way. They just tell her to dump Christianity and get a real life. An apology wouldn't hurt.

Do you think they will apologize?

I hope so. We all share a history together in that church, and we are bound together for eternity. I have begun to understand that eternity is now. The term *afterlife* is a bit misleading, because Christ has saved us and we are his people right *now.* It's sad, silly and sinful for us to judge one another and drive wedges. I know that we can't make heaven here on earth, but we can get a taste of it. It's not cumulative, though. For every step up, we slide back down. We just have to do what is right when it is revealed to us.

My kids knew Don, and I want them to see him as a brother in Christ who can be reconciled, even after death, to those sisters who couldn't understand his particular situation. If our kids can see us rise above the pettiness and hurt, then Don will smile and the angels will rejoice in heaven the way they do when a lost soul comes to Christ. That's what I believe, anyway.

16

I Killed the Barbie Doll He Gave Me

Now in her mid-twenties, she's the daughter of fundamentalist parents who came of age in the sixties. In talking with her I sense that culturally she is far removed from her parents. Her language and attitudes clearly mark her as a woman of the nineties, yet every now and then a term, a turn of phrase or a mannerism creeps into her conversation like the vestigial twang of a Texas drawl in a transplanted New Yorker.

She loves and respects her parents but has no desire to return to the fundamentalism of her childhood. She is interested in a workable Christian faith, however, and longs for a relationship with Christ that can survive the shifting sands of modern life.

She is particularly self-assured and speaks without hesitation, even when describing the violent sexual abuse she suffered before entering grade school, which precipitated her disenchantment with fundamentalism. When I speak with her, it's easy to see why she survived to triumph over obstacles that might have defeated someone else. She knows what she wants. She's just trying to figure out how to get it.

* * *

Both my parents are fundamentalists. I definitely am not. I'm a Christian, but I'm much more liberal. My parents and I went through some huge battles. Everything was one way or no way with them. Most of my friends chose not to believe any of the Christianity we were all raised with, but I have recently come back to my Christian faith after a time of rejecting.

I did the whole pop-culture book thing. I read *Codependent No More* and the rest of the self-help, human potential list. But after trying hard to heal myself, I looked at my life and realized that I could make choices based on my faith in Christ.

I was living with a guy, but it didn't feel right. Though he is a non-Christian, he was good to me. He wasn't abusive or anything, but premarital sex just wasn't where I wanted to be. I was searching for more than a secular life where I could make as few waves as possible. When you decide to let the chips fall where they may, they don't always fall well.

I wanted to live as a Christian. It was hard to break up with my boyfriend, because in a sense there was no reason to. I was changing the rules on him.

What made you want to "let the chips fall where they may"? It sounds like you sort of gave up on life for a while.

Not on life, but certainly on Christianity. My family had some awful experiences in churches. My parents should have gotten us out of there. At least that's what I say when I'm in my "blame-the-parents mode." *She laughs.* My father didn't provide a leadership role, and he and I have just recently come to an understanding.

When I was five my father's father raped me. He raped or molested all the girls in our family, and everybody knew about it.

There is a long pause as I process what she has just told me.

Let me clarify that. I'm sure my folks didn't know about him *before* he raped me. I didn't mean it that way. My grandma and aunts knew beforehand, though, because he had done it to the aunts.

My grandfather was a Sunday-school superintendent in a fundamentalist church. I was staying at his house, and it was my first time away from home. He asked me if I wanted to go out to the barn to see some kittens. That was the bait.

After he raped me, I knew he had done something very wrong, so I said that I was going to tell. He threatened to hurt me, hurt my parents and even hurt my baby brother, but I just said, "No! I'm going to tell."

Afterward my grandmother gave me a bath and cleaned me up, so she knew exactly what had happened. I got on the phone and told my mom, "You have to come and get me now!" I remember my grandfather sitting right there beside me during the call. He took the phone from me and told my mother that I was just making a fuss because I was away from home. "Nothing to worry about," he assured her.

Well, my parents came and got me. I started to tell them and my mom really lost it, so I didn't tell them the whole story. My grandfather tried to gloss it over. He bought me a Barbie doll, which I promptly and efficiently killed. I murdered that Barbie doll! *She laughs. She tells this story with the verve and confidence of someone who has worked through the deepest angst and is on the upswing.*

You killed Barbie? Girl, you are a backslider!

Yep! Pulled her hair out, ripped off her arms and legs. Smashed her head. I wasn't going to get bought off for a lousy doll! I still hate Barbie dolls to this day. I hate cats too.

But I'm sure that was when the whole church thing started to fall apart for me. The extended family, of course, rallied around my grandfather. "He did it to us and we're okay," the aunts whined. "Why do you want to make trouble?" *She shakes her head.* Actually they were far from "okay," as you can imagine. What a bunch of screwed-up women! My grandmother just said, "Satan's gotten to him again."

She said "again"?

Pathetic, isn't it? I still hold more anger toward my grandmother than I do toward him. You would think as a woman she would have a sense of what it's like to be raped.

Maybe she did.

Well, maybe so. People sure do react in strange ways. I still have trouble forgiving her for letting me come out to the house when she knew what was in store for me.

Often when fundamentalists sin, they say something to the effect that Satan wouldn't be trying so hard to trip them up if they weren't being successful for the Lord.

Ooooh! I know! That makes me want to kill. When I hear that I just start to lose it. Whatever happened to admitting guilt, asking for help and getting better? What a slimy, miserable cop-out that one is!

My father didn't press charges, partly because I didn't tell him the whole story and partly, I think, to avoid giving the church a bad name. Grandpa agreed to seek counseling, but after two sessions he stopped and decided to go into foreign missions work—with a children's ministry. God had called him, he said. That's why I don't exactly snap to attention when someone says God told them something. Yeah, right!

I shouldered a lot of guilt when I was growing up. I thought about that evil man set loose on all those poor kids. But as a child you don't know what you can do.

I didn't tell my folks he had actually raped me until much later, when I was in college. So for all those years, even though I hadn't told them the full story, I was processing everything I heard in church through what I had experienced. I was in my teens when I took control of the situation and started therapy.

Later my family decided to visit him. I hadn't seen him since he had raped me, and my folks were very good about it. They said that we didn't have to go, and that *I* certainly didn't have to. But I was a good girl, so I said, "Oh no, I don't mind." When we got there (he had moved after coming back from overseas), I saw that he had a garage that was a lot like the barn he had lured me into. I tried to put that out of my mind, but then the scumbag asked my little brother if he would like to go out to the garage to see some kittens. That bastard hadn't changed a bit. He even used the same line! I'll bet he didn't even remember that he had used it on me. He was a hard-core pedophile if there ever was one.

I stood up and said very angrily, "No, he won't be seeing any kittens today! In fact, we're all leaving right now!" I took my brother's hand

and I walked right out of the house. My parents followed. Once I started counseling, my therapist reported him to the police, so at least there's a warning out on him.

I sued him for the cost of therapy. I didn't want a cent more than that, so I just asked a lawyer to advise me, and then I wrote a letter spelling out what I felt I was owed for therapy fees. I started getting all these calls from lawyers, including one who said, "That was just an issue of pornography, not rape." He recounted the scenario in lawyerlike fashion, explaining why I wasn't really a rape victim. I said, "Excuse me, but that evil son-of-a-bitch doesn't even remember which one I am. I'm the one he *raped.* You are describing his molestation of some other little girl. It sounds despicable, by the way, but sorry, wrong girl." And they wonder why no one likes lawyers.

You seem to have a pretty strong sense of self. Many sexual abuse victims find themselves either emotionally shut down or angry and rebellious.

Well, I was never a froufrou girl. After I killed that Barbie doll, I stayed away from all that girlie stuff. I was a cheerleader in high school, though, and I was very popular. I have always been surrounded by lots of friends. I have always had strong opinions, and I have not been afraid to state them.

On the other hand, I was bulimic from age thirteen to twenty, so there was obviously a lot of internalized angst inside me. I get some of that from my mother, who comes from an enraged family.

An "enraged" family? That's an interesting turn of phrase.

Her upbringing was very abusive, although not sexually abusive. She doesn't cause trouble, but she seems to find it. She's learning to pick her battles, I think, as she grows wiser with age.

In her last church her pastor was a psychopath. I'm not using the term frivolously. The man was a megalomaniac who had to control everyone. My mother just stayed and kept trying to reason with him. My father did too, but Mom had more of a need to fix things. That may be a byproduct of her childhood, where she always had to live in fear. As an adult she wanted to stand her ground. It was excruciating to watch that pastor crucify my mother. He would keep making up new hoops for her to jump through. It was all about submission to his authority. I think that my brother and I were almost ready to take him out. That's not why you go to a church. Who needs it?

We were somewhat chaotic as a family when I was growing up. To this day we need to work on that. I wonder if it's because my parents were both raised by such control freaks. The result was that they gave me less structure, and that didn't work out for me. I got into too much trouble. Chaos.

My brother is the exception. He's the most organized, controlled person I know. He's younger than me and he owns a home. There isn't a cushion out of place either. But he's controlled, not a controller. There's a big difference.

My parents are in a really great church right now, and I'm happy for them. It preaches the gospel, and I would call it a fundamentalist church, although my mother wouldn't. But it's much more loving and open. The pastor preaches very candidly about his own temptations toward demagoguery and warns the congregation.

I still see it slipping more toward fundamentalist ways, though. I see it in their small group activities. Those little groups can become like microchurches in themselves. I have seen them get isolated and shut off.

That's what happened to a Christian school I went to. It was in a little country town, kind of a hippie town really. The fundamentalists came in and killed the school with their desire to have it be right on every issue. It wasn't all that bad of a place, even though you did have to hold up a little flag if you wanted to have your work checked or go to the bathroom. The fundamentalists didn't understand or respect the other families, and the school just died.

Fundamentalism is a way of thinking. One of my mother's sisters got involved in the Children of God for a while. That's a pretty wild cult that on the surface would seem like anathema to fundamentalists, but it's just another manifestation of the need to rally around a charismatic leader with all the "true" answers. An independent thinker with a sense of ambiguity wouldn't fall for that as easily.

The Children of God have been accused of institutionalizing sexual abuse of children.

I know. It's sad that a woman from an abusive home would find her way to an abusive cult leader. My aunt's family is out of that cult now, but they're in a very controlling fundamentalist church. So to me, at least, it seems like just more of the same.

I want a faith relationship with Christ, but I would rather crawl on my knees for ten miles than enter a joyless, spirit-crushing fundamentalist church like the ones I grew up in. I would no sooner go to a Bible camp or a youth rally than walk on the moon.

Still, I know that God is working in my life. It sounds funny to talk like that, but it sounds right too. I told you that I hated cats because of the way my grandfather lured me out to the barn. My new roommate has a cat that loves me. It's not just marking me with its scent either. It likes to be around me, sit on my lap, the whole works. I shove it away—actually I *throw* it away when no one is around. That cat can take some abuse! But now I find myself softening a bit in my attitude toward that cat, and toward cats in general. I still hate Barbie dolls, though.

I don't know exactly how it will work out, but I find myself being drawn toward God as the ragged edges of my life get repaired. That leaves me in an awkward position, because my boyfriend, who has no religious background, is a searcher. He was a searcher before we broke up, but now he is looking at Christianity and asking me all kinds of questions about the Bible. Oddly enough, even though I spent my whole childhood memorizing verses, I can't help him out. I have nothing to work with. Maybe I just blocked it all out or something.

What do I do if he gets saved and wants to go to church? On the one hand I would rejoice, because then we could have a chance at a life together. But I see a certain proclivity toward fundamentalist thinking in him that I don't like. He's a very logical (or maybe the word is sequential) guy, and he wants to know the answers.

That's what fundamentalism offers. It doesn't deliver it, but you can't know that if you haven't been raised in it. The whole business frightens me.

17

I Want to Feel His Pleasure

Before he died of AIDS several months after this interview, he struggled to make peace with his family and church, although his peace with God had been accomplished much earlier.

In one of several interviews, we meet in a funky local tavern that has been the favorite haunt of many writers, including one Pulitzer Prize winner. It's a smoky dive that began as a gas station in the 1930s and is now battling for a place on the historic register. Bikers, cowboys, frat types and businesspeople yell, play pool and carouse. We sit in a snug corner, tucked away from the commotion.

He drinks one beer during our long conversation, a locally brewed ale with enough malt and yeast in it to bake a loaf of bread. He's engaging, funny and deeply thoughtful.

In a previous interview he was wearing a blue power suit and looked every inch the businessman he was. Now he is dressed in jeans and a pressed shirt. He looks much younger than his thirtysome years and, well—more approachable.

* * *

I know what you're staring at. *He grins mischievously.* It's okay. My hair, right? I didn't have any last time we talked.

Well—you were . . .

Go ahead *(he laughs joyfully):* a cue ball! Now I sport this luxurious growth! I had two choices: a trip to Europe or hair. What vanity! I took the hair. *We both laugh.*

Part of my recovery has to do with accepting the way I look. I've always hated the way I look: my skinny legs, my prematurely shiny head. *(He's actually very handsome.)* I hated not only myself but my image in the mirror.

When I tested positive for HIV, I had to take stock of my life. How did I get where I was? I went to some counseling sessions at a local ministry that tries to help people who want out of the homosexual lifestyle. Part of what I had to do was slow down and figure out what I really thought of myself. That was hard. It's still hard. Now I have this virus, and that doesn't make it any easier.

Why did you get tested? Were you sick?

No. I just knew that the life I was leading exposed me to the danger of infection, and I wanted to know. I was living with a guy, but he doesn't want to get tested. A lot of people don't.

We had an open relationship, even though we were very close, and I would sometimes go to the bathhouses. Sex was very obsessive with me. I'm what is called a sex addict. In my more honest moments I knew that my addiction was way out of control and I was a danger to myself and others. Like all addictions, it is part of a larger spiritual problem that has to be addressed.

Was there a particular turning point for you in wanting to deal with the larger spiritual problem?

My parents, who had been growing increasingly distant from me, finally confronted me one day and just said, "We know something is very wrong. We love you and we want to help, but we don't know what it is that is troubling you."

So I dropped the bombshell. I said that I had been living as a homosexual for years and that I had HIV. They took it surprisingly well. They were hurt, but at that point I don't think they were too shocked because all the signs were there. They affirmed their love and support for me.

That sounds like a fairly positive turn of events, given that some parents disown their gay children.

Well, yes and no. We still have a long way to go. They have a faith that's very much based on do's and don'ts. They respond to most issues with dogma, and their idea of a Christian life is to be busy in church, have daily Bible readings and avoid certain sins. But they have a hard time expressing love. My mother is a very vibrant, upbeat person in many ways, but she can be quite judgmental. While growing up I was often struck by the kindness she could show in some situations and then the extreme hatred she could have for—well, homosexuals. My father is very successful and busy, and he has always been out of my reach.

There are a lot of theories about why some people are drawn to homosexual activity. One theory (and I think that it's true in my case) is that boys long for close male companionship if they lacked their father's love when they were children. Sometimes that becomes eroticized and manifests itself as homosexual attraction.

I have many friends who are openly homosexual and consider themselves both normal and Christian. I'm only speaking for myself. I never thought of myself as a homosexual. It was not a rewarding or satisfying life. In a love relationship between a man and a woman, they balance one another out. I know this will sound very regressive and stereotyped, but the man is the pursuer. The woman, because she is motivated differently, wants love and affection rather than just sex.

In most marriages the man can be satisfied by sex, without much romance or foreplay. The woman usually wants to be courted. Women take longer to become aroused. That forces heterosexual couples to defer to one another, to take time to please one another. And I'm told that out of that comes, or can come, a genuinely balanced love. But when men who aren't connected to any one person go after other men, the bathhouse scene is a frequent result. You just keep trying to find that closeness and satisfaction, but you're never really satisfied because you're just in an unnatural situation.

Again, not all people would agree with me, but it was true for me. Not all homosexual men go to bathhouses. Some seem to have longer-lasting, genuinely monogamous relationships. I was propelled by self-loathing. I would deny my homosexual urges and then go on these wild, obsessive binges. Then I would shut down and become Mr. Conservative Businessman with my three-piece suit and attaché case. If you had caught me leaving the baths at 4:00 a.m. and asked me if I was homosexual, I would have said no. And I would have believed it.

Your friends say that you were the model Christian young person as a kid. You were raised in conservative churches and did everything right. How did you go from that to the homosexual life you have described?

My first encounter was with another Christian kid in a youth group setting. We were on an outing and it just happened. He more or less initiated it. After that I avoided him like the plague. He later became quite open about his homosexuality and left the church. He was hanging out with older guys in the gay community and wearing makeup to school. I couldn't chance being associated with him because I was trying to live a conservative Christian life.

I tried to just forget that it had happened. Total denial. But now and then, with increasing frequency, I would have sexual binges. It was all very secret—in a sense even from me. I couldn't talk to any adult Christian about it, so it was all internalized. The denial worked pretty well for a long time.

Also, there are lots of men like me in the churches. We usually avoid one another for fear of exposure. In the homosexual subculture you learn to read eye contact and subtle gestures, especially back then when it was such an enormous taboo. You discern interest from other men in subtle ways. In a gay bar you might follow up on it, but in a Christian setting you have to squash it. What if that guy starts to feel guilty and in telling someone about himself he mentions you too? Besides, in the Christian setting you're trying to suppress your sexual side and pretend it doesn't exist.

It sounds like a very unhappy life. Did you ever think about just coming out and living openly as a gay man?

No. I don't think of myself as gay, or homosexual, or any other label. I don't want to live a homosexual life. Some heterosexually oriented Christian men have a lifelong obsession with pornography, prostitutes, other men's wives or even children. Not too many of them would tell you that they *want* to think of themselves as adulterers and build a lifestyle around it, even if it was a lifelong obsession. Usually in the deepest part of their heart they want to live another way, but they don't know how. Like me, they would be outcasts if they shared their struggles openly, so usually they get into double living and denial.

Again, some people do want to live as homosexual men, but I don't. My real desire is to fall in love with a woman and have the kind of Christian family that some people are able to have. I know that's a long shot at this point, though. Actually I have a girlfriend now. She knows that I am HIV positive, and that makes it hard to be intimate or have a sense of a future together.

You said that you were very involved in church and youth activities as a kid. Did you continue to go to church as an adult?

Not really. Church is designed for the nuclear family: Mom and Dad take the young kids. My experience has been that there is little room for single people, especially eligible single men who aren't dating women. There is quite a bit of pressure to get married, and that's hard to handle when you're having a promiscuous sexual life with men.

Did you ever think about just telling a pastor or youth pastor about your sexual life?

No. Actually most single heterosexuals wouldn't be truly honest about their sexual life with their pastor. Young unmarried couples who are sexually active probably wouldn't go in and ask the pastor to help them abstain from sex, because, in a sense, they want to keep doing what they are doing.

But for me it was deeper than that. I was in such strong denial that I couldn't even think about what I was doing sexually, except when I was doing it. I really was split into two people. That stress and shame and fear are probably part of what drove me into ever more reckless sexual activity. Besides, if I had told someone, I doubt that they would have known what to say.

I am involved in a group ministry with some other Christians now, and I can be very honest with them. *He laughs.* But we're all basket cases there. Even the leader, who is a highly respected Christian leader in our city, has a pretty dysfunctional relationship with his brother, who is also a highly respected Christian leader.

What makes this group work for you when other groups didn't?

None of us have any illusions. We all know how messed up we are. We actually believe what the Bible says: *all* have sinned and fall short of the glory of God. I did go to a church for a while. It's much more . . . I couldn't say liberal in the theological sense. It's much less enamored with illusions about its own holiness. As a result, it's actually more holy than the conservative churches that I grew up in, where they tried so hard to be holy and produced people like me. *We both laugh heartily. A waitress in a tie-dye dress asks if we would like another beer. He waves her off.*

Why did you stop going to that church?

This will be hard for a lot of people to understand, especially for those who see church attendance as pivotal to one's faith. Church is too painful. When I sit in a pew and go through the actions of singing, praying and hearing the sermon, it just hurts. It brings up all those years (most of my life, really) when I had to live a lie. It drives me toward those same impulses to lie, cover up and play games. I get physically sick.

Fellowship for me now is being with friends who can take me as I am. That's the way Christ takes me.

Can you tell me about your recovery therapy?

Sure. Again, I don't want people to read this and think that I'm making blanket statements. I could be completely wrong. I can't speak for every person who has been involved in homosexuality. Maybe I'll change my thinking at some point.

Promiscuous homosexual activity gave me this virus. But my problem, my deep spiritual condition, has little to do with that. A person can't solve this type of problem by just refraining from acting upon sexual urges.

My problem is the same as everyone's. I was separated from a loving relationship with Christ. Being involved in homosexuality made me a pariah in some people's eyes. It also made it more difficult for me to submit to Christ, because the church acts as if it owns Christ instead of the other way around. You don't have to fulfill the membership requirements of this or that denomination to be reconciled to Christ. You have to submit to Christ.

I have spent so much of my life trying to be something that I'm not, so now I have to be who Christ calls me to be. I'm tendering my resignation at work and going back to school to major in music. The businessman was never really me. My friends told me that, but I wasn't honest enough to hear it.

Your friends say that you have always been quite a musician. They recall you playing the piano in high school.

I wasn't a musician. I hardly knew one song all the way through. I took lessons, but it was so I could play accompaniment in church. I spent most of the time doing gags to make people laugh. I never learned to hear or experience music. Now I want to learn to hear music the way Christ hears it, not just as a means to an end.

In a subsequent interview, we meet in a café in a trendy area of town that is home to a large gay and lesbian population. Afterward we walk by a park known for anonymous homosexual encounters. It is a warm summer night. A gentle breeze rustles the lush canopy of oaks and maples above us.

A young man walks quickly from the darkness of the park and beeps his remote car lock as he glances furtively over his shoulder. He quickly enters a Saab convertible and drives off past the stately brick and stone houses for which the area is famous.

That was me a year ago. Quick, anonymous sex with a stranger, then I was out of there. Did he look like he was feeling good about himself?

No more or less than a lot of married men who have just left a nudie bar or massage parlor, I suppose.

That's a good comparison. I still see my old friends from my previous lifestyle. I don't tell them that since I'm born again and they're going to hell, we can't see one another anymore. I don't believe that.

I have told them what I'm telling you. Some of them are put off by my new direction. There's a sense that I'm just fooling myself and that I have betrayed the community, but most are actually very supportive because they know it's what I truly want.

We comment on the homes and gardens as we stroll. I point out a particularly graceful stairway and wonder aloud if the same concrete finisher might have done many of the other, similar stairways in the neighborhood.

You know, I would never have noticed that. My childhood was always focused on the practical, never the aesthetic. I know nothing of architecture, painting or sculpture. Like most fundamentalists, I'm a philistine. Art was learning to make posters at Sunday school.

An architect I know coined the term "evangelical drywall" to describe the bland, utilitarian style of most of our churches. He had been overwhelmed by the way the European cathedrals reflect the glory of God in their architecture, tapestry and windows. Sometimes I wish that I had been raised Catholic or Episcopalian so I could see and hear that way. He grew up appreciating Gregorian chants and other sacred music in a way that I am just starting to. In my tradition the words were the thing. Just the words.

How do your parents feel about your career change? Do they understand why you want to abandon a financially rewarding career in business for the tentative promise of a musician's life?

They try, but they don't really get it. And there's the question of how long I will live. People with HIV don't usually switch to long careers in anything.

It think that it was Luther who was asked, while he was hoeing a row of corn, "What would you do if you knew that Christ would return in the next hour?" He said that he would finish the row.

That's what I'm trying to do—what Christ has called me to do. I think it has something to do with music. I'm beginning to feel the joy of Christ when I play. I'm also trying to spend as much time as I can with my folks, because I want to really know them, and for them to know me.

In the movie *Chariots of Fire* Eric Liddell is asked why he spends so much time running, since he plans to be a missionary. He replies, "When I run I feel God's pleasure." I want to feel his pleasure.

Part 4

Family Values: Life with Father, the Rod of Correction, the Perfect Christian Family

18

Sin Was What Other People Did

He's a strong, quiet man in his mid-forties who is an active member of a mainline evangelical church and a father of young children. He is clean-cut, athletic and vibrant. But when we discuss his childhood, his eyes give away the pain that continues to be a part of his daily life.

When we get to the topic of this book (life in a fundamentalist family), he steels himself. His voice drops an octave, and his body tenses. This is a touchy, painful subject for him, loaded with spiritual and psychological land mines. Yet he is eager, perhaps driven, to talk about it.

We meet several times in person and then finish with a long telephone discussion. He is forthcoming and open, but he holds back at first, wondering how I will take what he has to say.

* * *

I was raised in a large fundamentalist church that was located in an established community in the city. I actually have many positive memories about being raised in the church. I can't speak of "that part" of my childhood, because my whole life was part and parcel of the fundamentalist church experience.

On the positive side, we really were one big happy family. At least when I was very young. We would go on big family picnics in the park. It felt very warm, very right. I also loved Vacation Bible School, which I went to from early grade school through junior high. We would put on massive parades for Jesus, where we would march through the streets with signs and banners. This was during the civil rights era, so street marches were very much a part of city life. This was *our* demonstration, and it was very positive and affirming.

I still have vivid memories of some of the old stalwarts of the faith, people my parents' age who are still active in that church.

But on the negative side, almost all of my male friends eventually abandoned the Christian faith. It started in the high-school years, and by the time they went to college they were gone for good.

How did the church people explain that?

I'm sure they saw it as the snares of a worldly society, but from my point of view it had more to do with the dogmatic legalism the guys were raised with. They hadn't been taught to think, and when new, attractive ideas came along they had no way to process them. They had been given such strict, narrow parameters that when they got a little bit of freedom they just went for it. By high school most of them were lost causes.

I started to experiment in my high-school years, but I had a bigger box than most of my friends. My parents were not quite as controlling as my friends' parents. Also, I was the youngest of several kids, and my folks had learned to relax a bit.

The most painful legacy from that time, though, is that I grew up without a meaningful relationship with my father. I know that the distance between my father and me isn't all the fault of the church. Some of it must be from his upbringing too, but the dysfunctional behavior was always given the stamp of religion: "This is God's way. This is my way. They are the same thing."

As I grew up I saw that his view of Christianity skewed his politics, relationships, community, *everything.* It was very mean-spirited and self-congratulatory.

We never talked. *He* talked. At the end of the day he would give his commentary on the day's events. Everything bad that had happened in the world was the fault of blacks, communists, women or minorities. His key verse was "Be ye not unequally yoked." He applied this to everything in life.

He and most of the other men I knew in the church had two themes: spiritual and political. They promoted a brand of right-wing fundamentalism that was very racist. My father holds those same views today.

I can see that I have been very influenced by my father's worldview. Every now and then, when dealing with my kids or my wife, I'll find myself reacting. Being motivated by fear. Not legitimate fear, but fear of the unknown, like my father was.

To this day my extended family is dysfunctional, and much of it stems from my father's view of life. The other kids were affected much more negatively than me because, as I said before, they had narrower boundaries.

In reality the boundaries didn't mean much for most kids, because they just went ahead and did what they wanted to do. My own rebellion was pretty tame in most respects. I never drank until I got to college, and then I didn't like it. I never danced. Never learned to. The first time I ever danced was with my wife. In the fifteen years we have been married I have danced three times.

He pauses, searching for the right words.

My rebellion—it was tame in most respects. Except in the sexual area. Then it was dangerous.

My brother has a sexual addiction, as do two of my other friends from that church. I don't know how much their spiritual upbringing is to blame for that, but in my years as a police detective I saw a lot of deviant sexual abuse perpetrated by children of fundamentalists. There are several scientific studies that point in this direction.

One of my Christian friends is an attorney, and he defends people accused of sexual abuse. He was shocked by the numbers of Christians who had committed sexual crimes against children. We talked about it. He was very disheartened by this.

I experimented with homosexuality for a couple of years when I was in college. I never really got into the homosexual culture, which I think can be very ensnaring, but I was drawn to it. I was rescued from that with relatively minor damage.

Why? What kept you from becoming more involved?

My own realization that it was wrong and my desire to keep away from it. I just didn't feel that I was homosexual, and I didn't want to be homosexual.

I have spent time in therapy over this issue. I had a good friend who prayed with me, and I was saved from some potentially destructive behavior.

This is hard to say, because it's so hard for people to understand. I hope this won't be taken the wrong way, but at times I would feel closer to God after an encounter with another man.

I think that's because after an encounter I would truly experience confession and forgiveness in a way that I did not at any other time. In my church there was a need to always appear wholesome, normal and perfect. Sin was what other people did. At least the big sins. We lived as though we were separate from the really "big" sins, which was of course not true.

Having gone through that experience of despair and forgiveness, and having met so many men who have shared that experience, I hate to see churches get on the antihomosexual bandwagon. There are men and boys in our churches who hear that cruel, condemning tirade and just emotionally withdraw. The church needs to be more humble and realize that our people struggle with all the things that other people struggle with. That's why I am so opposed to fundamentalist thinking. I have seen the damage it's done to brothers and friends.

My friend said that he sees a massive amount of compulsive behavior in fundamentalist circles. I'm inclined to agree. Christian fundamentalism is a cultural defense society. It's not about following Christ. They take rules and cultural norms that a certain group of people have grown up with and try to sanctify those norms as though they came from God.

We made a list of the "doctrines" that our fundamentalist churches had pushed and found that very few had any basis in Scripture. Some, like the overt racism, were directly contrary to everything Christ taught.

I was a police officer during all the unrest of the late sixties, and I was still in the fundamentalist church. One Sunday as I entered the sanctuary, a deacon pulled back his jacket and showed me the .25-caliber automatic he carried in a shoulder holster. He winked and whispered, "No black man is getting through these doors while I'm around here!"

I said, "Bobby! What do you mean?" I guess the shock and disgust must have registered pretty clearly on my face, because he pulled back. He realized that he had tipped his hand to someone outside the circle. And by then I *was* outside the circle.

But he was just following the same paranoid line of thinking that my father followed. He must have thought that black folks from the ghetto would come all the way down to our racist church in the white neighborhood and try to enter the sanctuary. Much of the so-called doctrine was just a ploy to keep everyone else away. It was all designed to protect our own narrow view of life.

Once when I was a young adult my father asked me, in my mother's presence, "Well, how did we do raising you?"

I was going through some real inner turmoil, and he caught me off guard. I didn't know what to say. There was a long, awkward pause. He finally said, "I'm sure we made mistakes, but anyone watching from the *outside* knew we were a good family."

What he meant by "people watching from the outside" was other people in the church. He didn't worry about us kids, he just wanted to present a good façade to the other people.

But my brothers and I suffered a great deal. One of my brothers would tell you that everything is fine, even though he has two kids and is divorced because of his sexual problems. His girlfriend told me once, "Your brother's penis runs his life!"

Another brother pastors a very bizarre church. I'm not even sure of the name—we don't see each other much. (And when we do we can't really talk.) It's a weird mix of Eastern and Western philosophies. He would say that he has moved away from fundamentalism, and he has—in terms of religious doctrine. But he's as legalistic and paranoid as my father. He has maimed all his kids. They live a hand-to-mouth existence, and they're socially dysfunctional. They're nice kids, but they have a hard time living their lives.

My folks spent so much energy trying to look like a "good" family, but it turned out badly for everyone. I have been in therapy, and my wife is very supportive, so I am doing better than the others. I have been completely open with my wife about my past.

But two of my siblings totally rejected the Christian faith, and three others are all in some kind of legalist environment. The funny thing is that my father doesn't see any of his grandchildren as successful except mine, and we're the ones who have become what he would call liberals or backsliders.

Why does he see your kids as successful?

We were always solicitous. My wife and I wanted to break the legacy of dysfunction, so we just kept making time for the kids to see their grandparents. Even though I disapprove of the things my father may say to the kids, I want them to know their grandparents. I don't want my kids to be yet another generation of our family who can't talk to one another or love one another.

My brothers' kids are standoffish. I think my brothers talk Dad down in front of them. That kind of backbiting just poisons the whole family.

How does a parent break that cycle of paranoia and guilt?

I know my wife and I have made mistakes, and we'll make plenty more, but we decided to learn from our peers. We looked at families who have raised their kids into the teen years without driving them off or making them crazy.

What we discovered isn't too surprising. The ones whose kids are loving and strong in the faith, or at least open to the faith, tend to be people who give their kids broad boundaries. They are firm about two areas: if God's Word specifically says it's wrong, or if it's physically dangerous. They tell their kids not to be harmful, then they give them a pretty big playing field.

We have tried to learn from those people. We have also tried to learn to have a respectful, ongoing dialogue with our kids. We don't want to just lecture them like my father did. Rather, we want to listen as well as talk, taking time to hear them and then give loving guidance.

I'm sure my folks and their fundamentalist friends had good motives, but they did a lot of harm because they couldn't learn from outside their own little circle.

How would you deal with a child who was having homosexual feelings? What might have helped you work through the feelings you were having as a young man?

I was not consciously aware of homosexual feelings as a kid. It's hard to talk about, because I'm not sure today what went on. I don't believe that I was born that way, and I don't believe that any one person caused me to have homosexual feelings.

As I look back, I know that I so desperately wanted my father's approval. I needed the love of a man. In high school I had a very positive male bonding experience with a teacher. He was a kind and loving role model. I also had some positive male bonding with some friends.

In high school I went to a party where there was some—I guess you would call it sexual showing off. It didn't feel right, but it was very intriguing to me at that time. However, I felt that some line had been crossed morally. One of the guys who was more into it said, "There's lots of this going on at Lincoln Park down by the river." I didn't act on that knowledge, and I didn't get involved again until a couple of years later, when I was in college.

I had lived near that park as a kid. I used to play there. I had no idea that it was a place for homosexuals to meet and have encounters.

Well, I eventually went there and found it very tempting. I was inquisitive, and I did have some encounters, although, like I said, I didn't really get drawn into the subculture. But it was a place where I could meet men who would let me act out my sexual showing off and say, "You're good."

I came very close to falling into that whole subculture. There was drama and danger, and it was all very intriguing. I've got some pretty ugly stories that I'm not proud of.

That was a very confusing time. It's still hard to remember it with much clarity, because I was so confused at the time. I do know that there was absolutely no one I could talk to in my church circle. I could never have said, "Dad, I'm having these sexual feelings for other guys."

After that time I think I was probably trying to find male love and acceptance in my work. I was a radio announcer, which back then was very male-dominated. I got a lot of affirmation from that role. A very important public official asked me to work out with him a couple of times a week, to keep on my good side. That was very heady stuff.

When I became a cop, that was also an almost completely male environment. It was very macho, and looking back I think that was a huge motive.

Interestingly, I was assigned to the biggest gay neighborhood in the city, including the park where I'd had my homosexual encounters, but I had no problems. I met lots of gay people there and got along well with them, but I was no longer drawn to them sexually.

I have since talked with many men like myself who grew up with no significant man in their lives, or who were rejected by the men in their lives. We have very similar stories. I have sought out friendships with older men I respect, and that's been very positive.

Some psychologists theorize that extreme sexual repression later manifests itself in deviant and destructive sexual behavior. What do you think about that?

That does seem to play a role. I'm part of a healing prayer team in our church. People come to us for prayer when they want healing. I've had four men come to me for prayer about problems with sexual addiction. These were men who had homosexual compulsions. They came to me on their own, and that was before I became more open to some of my Christian friends about my own problems with homosexuality.

This caused me to see that I wasn't alone. I think there are many men in churches who are ambiguous about their sexuality, but they haven't been given an invitation to seek counseling. Like me, they've had to stumble around on their own. I know how isolated and lonely that is.

How can people in the churches be more open and accepting of men who are struggling with homosexuality?

It's so important for churches to refrain from denouncing people as evil. I would agree that homosexual acts are immoral, just as many heterosexual acts are (such as adultery). But the message I got was this: even people who have doubts about their sexuality are evil. Not evil in the sense that we are *all* evil, but beyond that—tainted and marred by a particularly disgusting and unforgivable sin.

That's why I wouldn't have *dared* to ask my father or anyone else for guidance. It has been said that Christians are an army that shoots their own wounded. It sure was true in my case.

The church should be very careful about getting into antigay politics. Many people in the church struggle with their sexual identity. If they hear venom and hatred, as though only terrible sinners would think about homosexuality, they will be driven away like I almost was, and like so many men have been.

The church should teach sexual morality, but it shouldn't make people believe that they are horrible and disgusting if they have sexual thoughts. Too often the church comes across as antisex, and people have to find out about sex without any real guidance.

I'll give you an example. When I was a kid I shared a bathroom with my brother. One night I heard my brother taking a bath, and my father walked in on him. My dad just screamed at him, "What are you doing?" Well, I'm sure he was masturbating. Boys masturbate. Dad just went into a rage and yelled, "That's wrong! I want you to *never* do that!"

Humiliating a kid and then giving him a moral absolute as though he has just murdered someone isn't going to teach him much about sin and grace. But that's the kind of experience that seems so typical of the way we were taught.

19

Creeping Fundamentalism

She's a former California beach girl. Now in her forties, she's married to a pastor, her childhood sweetheart. In the past year she has seen all her hopes and dreams evaporate. Her children have rejected her faith, which led the church elders to discipline her husband for being a rotten parent. The leadership of the church has, in her view, made a tragic situation even worse. Where she expected comfort and support, she found judgment and condemnation.

When I approach her about an interview, she is very willing to talk. Throughout our discussion she is on the verge of tears. Often she cries.

Her attitude is not marked by finger-pointing and anger, however. More than anything, she reminds me of a child who has been snubbed by all her friends or who is lost in a dark forest. She is deeply hurt, and she is confused, like a character in a Kafkaesque nightmare.

* * *

This has been the hardest, most painful and most disastrous year of my life. All I ever wanted to be in life was a Christian mother and wife. My only real goal was to raise up a Christian family, but now it is all evaporating. Our two oldest kids are hardened against our Christian values. My daughter left home and is pregnant (the father is not a Christian). My son is less rebellious, but he has no interest in Christ. Our younger kids are soft. They just don't want to be involved because of all the hurt and turmoil.

Our church has turned on us because of our daughter's rebellion. My husband is so discouraged he recently said, "I'd just as soon die right now." And he is a strong, committed man.

We read all of Dr. Dobson's books, went to Bill Gothard's seminars and did everything we thought we were supposed to do, yet it seems to have amounted to nothing.

It has been thirty years since I accepted Christ at my friend's fundamentalist youth group. I started going because there were some cute boys. I was a sixties teenager with some nominal church background but no understanding of the gospel. I met my husband in that youth group. He came to Christ there when he was fifteen.

The youth pastor was a popular, dynamic leader. We were confused teenagers brimming with questions. He had all the answers. One of our questions was "Where should a Christian go to college?" He insisted on a certain Southern fundamentalist school, and we all went there as a big lump. I never questioned his wisdom, even though our parents thought we were crazy.

My husband's folks in particular said, "What are you doing? There's no money in ministry." But he went off with ten dollars in his pocket and worked his way through. He has always been committed to a life of ministry.

The college was a total environment, with very strict rules about dress, dating and attendance. We heard all of the big-name fundamentalist preachers. It did have a lot of plays, musicals and visiting performers, though, so it wasn't really a deprived environment. They even had an excellent art collection. I felt okay about the school atmosphere, but my husband had misgivings about the legalism from the early stages.

Since we graduated thirty years ago, we have seen a lot of classmates just discard the whole thing. A great many alumni are embittered and alienated.

After graduation my husband decided to go to a theological seminary in the South that our church and college considered liberal. They thought nearly everyone else in the world was liberal, and the pastor told my husband, "If you go to that seminary, you will be useless for the Lord."

We had gone to their college of choice without the financial or emotional support of our families, and now the church more or less disowned us when we went off to an unacceptable seminary. Our ties were cut with that church from that time on.

I was glad we went to that seminary, though. I quickly saw that it had a more balanced, nonjudgmental approach. After seminary my husband taught for many years at a Bible college. Then we came to our present church, where he is one of several pastors.

Although we distanced ourselves from hard-core fundamentalism, I see now that there is a fundamentalist mindset that goes beyond denominational labels. I guess I would have to admit that I have some residual fundamentalist attitudes that are hard to get rid of.

We have a son in his twenties, a daughter who is about to graduate from high school and two daughters in grade school. We were probably a bit too strict with the two older kids, so we have modified our approach with the younger ones—but we have never been a family dominated by rules. We have always set standards about movies, music and behavior, but we have also talked with our kids and haven't just laid down an inflexible list of dos and don'ts.

I just don't know. *Her voice chokes up.* Even though I know what life is like, I guess I still cling to some of the idealism of fundamentalism. Two plus two will always equal four. There was security in that.

Somehow the fundamentalism you describe seems out of character for the stereotypical southern California beach girl of the sixties. What led you to desire this kind of security when the whole thrust of the youth culture was in the opposite direction?

I had gone to a Sunday school as a child, and I knew how to be a good girl even though I didn't hear the gospel. By sixth grade, though, life started moving pretty fast. In southern California a public-school girl is an adult by seventh grade. That was true even back then. It's not so much a life of freedom as it is a fast train ride. You get taken along whether you want to go or not.

A Catholic girlfriend of mine had started going to the fundamentalist youth group because there were boys there and it wasn't such a fast crowd. We could socialize without getting dragged into things we didn't really want to do. I was bothered by everyone asking me, "If you die tonight will you go to heaven or hell?" but it was a fairly comfortable place.

Once I accepted Christ and also accepted that fundamentalist mindset, there was a sense of relief. I knew what to wear, how to talk and what not to do with boys. It provided a very strong sense of security at that age. I made some good friends, and we really did have fun together. By the time I was sixteen or seventeen I knew I wanted to raise a family with that same sense of security and solid values. Now I look at my life and wonder, "How did we end up here?"

We were first-generation Christians, fueled by a burning desire to go all the way for Christ. Our kids have always had a take-it-or-leave-it attitude at best. They like the security (they will often ask us to pray for them) but not the commitment.

Our oldest son has even said, "I would like to have the faith you and Dad have, but I don't know how to get it." A friend once said, "Your son is a good man, but he's not a godly man." He doesn't want to have to *do* anything for the Lord.

Our oldest daughter, on the other hand, is like a character out of a soap opera. She is a cheerleader and was homecoming queen this past year. She will graduate from high school in a few weeks, and then she will be married. Then, in a couple of months, she will be a mother.

In junior high school she experienced the usual teen rebellion, typically involving minor matters like curfew and music. But by high school she had just written us off as far as parental authority. In her senior year she didn't want any rules whatsoever, and one day she just didn't come home from school. We thought she would eventually come back, but she had moved in with her boyfriend.

Is her rebellion tied to church activities or doctrines?

No. Our church is very relationship-oriented. It's theologically conservative, but we don't make rules about dress, music and movies. She just doesn't want God's will in her life. Sometimes I wonder if the gospel in our church is too easy, too focused on what Jesus will do for us and not enough on sacrifice. Maybe we went too far the other way. I don't know.

It's hard, because she doesn't talk to us, and so we have to hear everything through friends. She told a friend that her life is too laid out, that she doesn't want to be a "goody two-shoes," go to a Christian college and become a good Christian woman. She did tell me once that she had deliberately set her mind to go the other way.

I don't think that we ever verbally laid out a planned life for her, but even if we did, the one she describes sounds better than the one she's got now. We drive an old, beat-up Chevy Nova that we have owned since seminary. My husband said to her, "God wants you to have a Mercedes life and you're settling for a Chevy Nova." She just said, "Fine, I'll take the Nova."

She was caught shoplifting once, and then she got more and more sneaky and dishonest. We told her that we wanted to treat her more like an adult but that she was acting like a child and forcing us to regress and treat her like a child.

She became very angry and spiteful in her language and was having a destructive influence on our three younger kids, especially one sister who really adores her. She told a friend that she was pushing us because she knew we would eventually throw her out. My husband told her, "We would never throw you out. We might place you somewhere else if you are hurting the younger kids, but we would never throw you out on your own. We love you."

When she left home she moved in with her boyfriend and his mother, who has a live-in boyfriend. At first she got lots of affirmation there. The boy's mother told her that we were destroying her life and that we were crazy. But three weeks later the boy's mother kicked her out for lying and being disrespectful.

You said that the church turned on you over this. How did that come about?

We needed someone to weep with us, but the senior pastor and elders told us, "We're going to fix your broken family, and here's how." They had lots of advice, but they never asked us anything. They just figured they knew everything about us.

A woman from the church took our daughter in and said, "I'll fix your broken family." Two weeks later she dumped our daughter's clothes in the driveway and yelled from the window of her car, "It's time you grew up and started behaving like parents."

She had called my daughter at work and told her that I had come and taken her stuff, so now my daughter calls me up and starts berating me for interfering in her life. I told her what really happened, but she got her stuff and moved into an apartment with her boyfriend.

My husband had just gotten out of the hospital and was recovering from surgery when the elders decided to have him removed from preaching and counseling. They stood on the passage in the Bible that says a man must be the master of his home. They never asked me, or our kids, if he was a good husband or father. They just said, "If a tree bears bad fruit, that's your answer. We're just looking at the fruit."

My son, surprisingly, was furious. He was much more angry than I was. He went to the elders and said, "What's my dad supposed to do? He's done everything to bring me and my sister to the Lord, but we've chosen not to. We are people with a free will. How can you blame my father?"

Did the deacons discuss this with you before they made their decision?

No. That's what hurt so much. They met by themselves and listened to gossip. They had heard a story about my husband dragging my daughter around the house by her hair. Some kid told the youth pastor, and he told the elders. That incident never happened, but it was one of the "fruits" they talked about.

I can see now that many of the attitudes that caused us to leave strict fundamentalism are present in our church. Our youth pastor is very proud of his son, who loves Bible study and basketball and football—the model preacher's kid. My son asks questions. He's not a jock. Youth-group activities in our church aren't really geared for someone with his interests or temperament. For example, he would call me up after seeing a brutal massacre on television and ask, "Why all this evil? Where is God?"

So he wasn't out playing baseball or hollering at some youth activity. Does that mean he's a bad kid? The youth pastor seemed to think so.

I've been guilty of pride. My sister is still in a very strict fundamentalist church that continues to hurt her, and I have always taken pride that we served a more loving, supportive body. I guess I looked down on the no-smoking, no-dancing fundamentalists. But we're still trapped in a system of arbitrary rules and judgment ourselves.

My sister's son was class president of his Christian school, which expelled him three weeks before graduation. He had gone there since kindergarten.

What did he do to get such a harsh punishment? Was he dealing drugs to the other students or something?

No socks and no shave. They have a demerit system for tardies, behavior problems, dress codes and the like. He was late to school, so he jumped into his clothes and arrived a few minutes late. The secretary said, "You have to shave and put on some socks before you can go to class. You can't come to school looking like that." He replied that he would be even later if he drove back home for socks and a shave, and he didn't want to miss important class time. Well, he and the secretary argued, and he was flippant, so she gave him demerits for dress code, personal hygiene, tardiness and attitude. That pushed his demerit total over the limit, and he was expelled. The demerit system is like a checkbook ledger. It's the numbers that make the difference. He's so angry he doesn't even know if he believes in God anymore. My sister is devastated.

For the past few months I have taken the younger kids to other churches. That has shown me that we were too ingrown in our church. Our elders aren't well grounded in the Scriptures, so they seem to make up rules as they go. They should have sought some kind of outside counsel before judging my husband the way they did.

We were in a rut and I didn't know it. It has been good to experience the other side of the fence and see a church that is normal and right before God, and to also realize that their practices coincide with our family's peculiar way of doing things.

They allowed my husband to resume preaching when our daughter turned eighteen. Though pregnant and living with her boyfriend, she was legally an adult and therefore not in my husband's house. So one day he is a terrible, incompetent father and the next day it is a dead issue.

But the damage had been done, and there was still a lot of flak from people in the congregation. On the other hand, I have over one hundred cards of support on my refrigerator door, all from people who say they understand and are praying for us.

That's unusual. In many cases like this people just turn their backs. I don't mean to downplay the negative response, but all those cards indicate a wellspring of support.

Almost every one of those cards is from someone who wrote that they too had children who rebelled and caused them heartache. I guess it's easy to judge when you haven't had to go through it. Many of the elders have very young children, so they don't really know what the future holds.

How is your husband taking it at this point?

This is the lowest point of his life. Our daughter got sick, so she came home. But as soon as she was well, off she went again. Her little sisters don't understand why she isn't living at home. The older son won't talk to her. The grief my husband feels over the children is compounded by the sense of abandonment by the church. He's put fifteen years into this church, and he's been highly respected and sought out. Now it's just assumed that he's an incompetent father and husband.

A lot of the stress came from my husband trying to pastor the elders who were treating him this way. He asked them, "If my daughter's actions disqualify me, what requalifies me?" This wasn't just for him, but for others who might later be in similar situations. "Must she become a Christian, move back home, get married, turn a certain age?" While we were trying to heal our family, they hindered us by arguing over the situation for months without a clear direction.

At first they said that my husband was emotionally distressed and couldn't be trusted to make sound judgments. Well, anyone would be emotional. They could have supported him instead of heaping more stress and uncertainty on him.

Some of the elders pointed out that the biblical qualifications for leadership are ideals and that nobody lives up to them every day of their lives.

Then they were going to make an announcement about my daughter, that she had run away and was living with her boyfriend. I asked them if they planned to talk to her first. They hadn't thought of that, so my husband had to remind them that the Scriptures teach that we should go to the person—first alone, then with others, then with the elders—before publicly announcing an excommunication to the whole congregation.

So did they go to her and talk to her?

They called her at work. But they also told her that they would be removing my husband from preaching and counseling. She called us up to talk to us about it, but we hadn't heard. They told our teenage daughter before telling us, and this was while my husband was fresh out of the hospital recovering from surgery.

Before he went into the hospital, they had told my husband that no decision had been made, or would be made, affecting his duties. After they blurted it out to our daughter, they asked us to meet with them in a restaurant, and then, with the waitresses and busboys coming and going, gave him a letter explaining it. I just had to walk out.

Later we found out that half of the elder board hadn't been informed or even consulted. Some of the other elders got the whole board together and told these guys, "You've bungled it."

Did you ever consider just leaving the church completely?

Many times. But we had given fifteen years of our lives to that congregation, and it was on the verge of a split over this. My husband met with each of the elders individually, trying to build some trust, but there had been so many arbitrary decisions that it was pointless.

If we had left, we would have given up our salary, housing and medical care, all while my husband was going through surgery. He also would have had to abandon his Ph.D. work. We didn't want to make a hasty decision that would have had that kind of extensive impact, especially given our state of mind.

One elder, a young man with small children, asked me, "Don't you think we can be the voice of God for you as we try to help you fix your family?"

I said, "No. Has the Holy Spirit left me along with my daughter? You listened to rumors and made arbitrary decisions that made a tragic situation worse. You never asked me anything before you made enormous decisions about my life. Of course you can't be the voice of God for me!" He didn't take that too well.

I asked him why he thought his kids were doing well at this point, and he said, "The grace of God." I replied, "Exactly. So are my kids where they are because of me?"

Teachers often meet parents who brag about one kid and blame the schools for the other one. It sounds like your elders only believe in God's sovereignty when things are going well.

They haven't spent much time reading Job. We have a quiet legalism creeping into our church that is much like the fundamentalism at our college. It's not talked about much, but it seems that it's becoming the mode of operation.

My husband has returned to all his duties, and he has determined before God to make it work. I can't go back to everything I was doing. At least not yet. I'm not ready to be the totally involved pastor's wife. I was the director of the children's choir, the head of the missions committee and the wedding coordinator.

After all those years of helping people in the church plan their weddings—decorating the hall, getting them dressed and so forth—it's ironic that I will be going to my daughter's wedding somewhere else. I had looked forward to her marrying a believer in our church. Now I will have a son-in-law who mocks my faith and whose mother will speak ill of our character to anyone who will listen. In a few months a grandchild will come into all of this. It's not what I thought life would be like.

I have been immersed in this for almost a year now, and I just feel that I can't catch up. My daughter wants everything to be fine. We're going to her wedding, and she wants to just move on from there. I don't want to dwell on the past, but I'm so overcome by the idea that she has settled for a meager life.

I don't understand why the God we have served all of our adult lives means nothing to our children, but I know that life isn't over yet. All I can say is, "You are God, and life is better with you than without you. I don't like a thing you're doing, though." *She laughs tearfully.*

I know it's foolish for me to be arguing with God. I remember when Job said the same sort of thing and God replied, "Where were you when I laid out the heavens?" I can't understand a bit of it. The hardest part is seeing the faith of our other children suffer because of all of this.

We have a teenager living with us, a new Christian from a troubled family. He said to me, "If I wasn't living with you and just a member of the church, I would wonder why anyone needs this. These elders are godly men who read the Bible and pray, and then *this* is what they come up with? My parents wouldn't treat anyone this bad, and they're unbelievers!"

I had big plans to show him life in a Christian home. If he comes out of this with any faith, it will be purely by God's grace. It sure won't be due to anyone's example that I can see.

Maybe this will show me more of God's grace. I know that I've learned how much legalism and pride we had that we didn't even know about. I've learned that I still have that knee-jerk fundamentalist impulse that tells me I have to pray, witness and earn God's love. A friend recently told me, "Remember that God couldn't love you more in the future than he loves you now. He already loves you totally." That went against all my impulses. I know that I react by subliminally asking what more I can do to win his favor.

Maybe if you talk to me in a year or two, I will have some sense of what this is all about. I have the feeling that I'm learning, and I know God loves me. I just can't put it all together. It's like I'm in a dark fog.

20

We Apologized to Our Kids

She's a pastor's wife in her late forties—a bright-eyed people person. It's easy to imagine her engulfed in the myriad activities of her small church.

But while she is friendly and energetic, she lacks the fervent perkiness of someone who parrots the theologically or socially correct line. She has about her the earnest, steady body language of one who has been through the fire. It's like the cautious, self-effacing confidence of a veteran who has seen combat.

Raised in what she describes as a militantly fundamentalist church in southern California, she followed her high-school sweetheart to one of the nation's most staunch fundamentalist colleges in the Deep South.

Now, with grown children, she looks back on her life as a fundamentalist pastor's wife with much self-searching. Still solidly evangelical in her beliefs, she no longer considers herself a fundamentalist.

* * *

We went through some very hard times with our oldest son. He was heavily involved in drugs and the drug culture, and he was very angry. He's a committed Christian now, but our younger son isn't. Our daughter has been much easier to raise, but that may be partly because we had to reevaluate the fundamentalist culture that taught us how to raise our boys.

I know that we went through all of this for a reason, because I find myself talking to so many people who are facing similar trials. When things were really bad with our oldest, I was so distraught that I had to question everything I had ever believed. I wondered if the Bible was even true. It has been a long process of sorting out the false teachings from the truth of God's Word.

We were raised in militant fundamentalism. Over and over we learned that if we would stay married, love one another and spank our kids, then our kids would turn out okay. But guess what? It's just not true. We did all that and we went through hell.

I remember standing on the proverb that says if you train up a child in the way he should go, when he's old he won't depart from it. It was used to justify the militant fundamentalist line, and we never questioned the way it was interpreted. Actually one of my husband's seminary professors tried to explain to us that it really wasn't a guarantee for trouble-free childrearing, but we weren't listening. We just never expected our kids to rebel.

The years our oldest son was into drugs were a terror. We daily feared for his physical safety. When he came back to the Lord and began the healing process, he wrote us a letter that said, "I've made the choices. My problems are my own." He took ownership for doing what he did—the drugs and everything that goes along with that life. But later he called me and said, "Mom, I've met people who never rebelled. I wonder why that is." He wants to explore that with us.

Our second son is not a Christian. He says that he just can't live that straight Christian life. I asked him why. I wanted to know what we had done to give him the impression that the Christian life couldn't be lived. He said that it was about sex. He said that he simply couldn't live without sex until he was married, therefore he couldn't be a Christian. So he lived with his girlfriend for two years before they married.

How did your sons' rejection of the Christian life affect your roles as pastor and pastor's wife in the church?

I have to hand it to the congregation, they never criticized us. Or if they did, I never heard about it. But I never felt that they knew or cared about what we were going through. We didn't really talk about it either.

We've had several friends—pastors and laypeople—whose kids have gone through really tough times, and it's the same for them. Either their churches don't talk about it, or they penalize them. There's not a kind or helpful spirit when your family is in crisis.

My husband and I both went to the flagship of fundamentalist colleges down South, and it has been hard to watch what has happened to some of our classmates. We were assured that if we followed the rules everything would work out.

One very close friend lost her husband to cancer when he was twenty-nine years old. Her church told her, "You are a Christian. You don't need counseling." She was devastated. She called me and said, "I'm a twenty-five-year-old widow. I lost the love of my life to a painful disease, and they say I don't need any counseling! I don't know what to do." She got to where she hated Christians, and now she doesn't consider herself a believer.

Fundamentalism is a distortion of the gospel. It's a list that you are told to follow as though it came off the mountain with Moses. The last ten years of our lives have been a process of throwing out the distortions and keeping the true Christianity. We tried the list, but the list didn't work. It didn't work for our friends either.

When things were really bad with our son, we attended a fellowship for pastors. We tried to share our problems and get some counseling, but the only thing the pastors and their wives could do was tell us about the wonderful kids they had. We got no encouragement whatsoever, and I was about to go crazy.

I just told my husband, "Get me out of this place now!" He was playing horseshoes and didn't realize how agitated I was, so he said he wanted to finish his game. I walked toward the car, and a woman we had known a long, long time approached me. She sensed how much I was hurting, and she stopped me. I just said, "I'm out of here!" and turned away, but she told me to hold on, and ran and got her husband.

Then the two of them poured out *their* story. Their son was a coke addict. He had robbed them six times and had done time in prison. The husband said he had gone to the top of a mountain and asked if God even existed. I had known them all those years, and this was the first I had ever heard about it!

That conversation brought a lot of healing, because it was the first time anyone was real with me. They were completely transparent, and that helped me to realize that I wasn't alone. It allowed me to take stock of the way I had been living. My husband and I began to question everything we had ever believed.

And you emerged as believing Christians?

More than ever. We began to see how inconsistent we had been. We'd said we believed all these things in the Bible, but we didn't live it very effectively. We really ignored the fruits of the Spirit—self-control, humility, kindness.

After you talked to the other couple about their son's problems, how did you change the way you related to your son?

I realized that we hadn't tried hard enough to keep communication open. We tried, but not hard enough. When my younger son moved in with his girlfriend, I didn't want to criticize him over and over like I had with his older brother. So after I spoke my mind I tried to say nothing. I thought that by not saying anything I would be giving him some breathing room or something.

Then my older son, who was by that time a Christian, told me that I needed to talk to his brother. I said, "I have."

He said, "No, Mom, you haven't. He feels rejected because you won't talk to him. He doesn't even feel like he can come to the house. Not criticizing isn't the same as talking. You have to *talk* to him."

So instead of just talking *at* him, I sat down and opened my heart. I told him what I had been feeling. I shared my fears and my hurt.

It turned out that he had been feeling rejected because I had stopped talking to him. I let him know that I would always love him. I promised him that I wouldn't pressure him about spiritual things. I'm glad that we talked, and I am grateful to my older son for encouraging me. The younger one still isn't a Christian, but at least we can be open with one another. I'm not saying that it has changed anything as of yet, but I believe it was the right way to respond.

The funny thing is, I asked the younger one if he was happy in his life of freedom. He admitted that he wasn't. If I had nagged him he never would have admitted that. It gives us the chance to be honest with one another. You can't expect your kids to be honest and open if you are closed and putting on a mask all the time.

My brother is going through a similar time with his daughter. She's pregnant and unmarried, so he has just shut her out. There's not a lot of connection between his words and the way he behaves. He has refused to help her with money. He has made her unwelcome in his home. He says that if he accepts her, it will send a message to his other kids that sin is okay.

I know where he's coming from, and I'm afraid I might know where he's headed. When you think in terms of a list, it's easy to shut people out when they don't measure up. But that's not what the Christian life is about. I didn't want to lose my children because they wouldn't conform to what I wanted.

I know a pastor in the same situation who refused to go to his daughter's graduation. There's a tendency among fundamentalists to withdraw love, money, recognition or support when someone makes a mistake. We were guilty of that to some degree. We had the list, and when our kids messed up we punished them.

Now when I look back I can see that everything we did backfired on us. We didn't want our kids growing up in southern California, so we moved to a little Midwestern church in a small town. We figured the wholesome community experience would be good for them. My oldest son told me that the move was very hard for him and that he never felt like a whole person there.

Because we wouldn't let him go to the arcade to play video games—that was on the list—he couldn't fully participate in his friends' activities. Little things like that worked against what we were trying to do for him, but we couldn't see it at the time.

He went to a very small Christian school, while the other kids in our church went to the big public school. In Little League all his teammates were from the public school. Public schools and their athletic departments are big stuff in the Midwest, so his self-concept suffered because he was always on the outside.

So we decided to move to a city in the South where he could go to a bigger Christian school, and that's where he first saw drugs. There was a lot of hypocrisy in that school, so we finally let him go to the public school.

After six weeks in the public school he wanted to go back to the Christian school. He was crying. But we told him that he had made a choice and he would have to stick with it. I guess we thought it would build his character and give him backbone. Now I can see that despite the Christian school's flaws he did have a support group there, and he probably would have been better off returning.

I'm not trying to beat myself up over this, but our best-laid plans didn't work. I'm learning that the Christian life isn't based on doing the "right" thing or following a list. Sometimes we don't know what the right thing is, and having a list of behaviors to check off just confuses things.

Now our daughter, who went through the same schools and same family as the boys, has a vibrant testimony and a real heart for the Lord. She prospered in the Christian schools, and she was a witness in the public schools. So what was different? It wasn't something "out there." It was largely us.

She and my oldest son both go to a Christian college in California that I would have considered far too liberal a few years ago. It's right out there near Sin City, yet they are living the victorious Christian life we hoped and prayed for all those years.

Looking back at your fundamentalist college experience, how do you feel about what you were taught?

She laughs. It was fake Christianity. There, I said it. Back then we told people that we needed the discipline. Our church saw that college as the *only* place for a Christian. It had discipline, all right, but it was *their* discipline. We just accepted all their rules without having to think for ourselves. Afterward, when I realized what a fake it was, I felt very angry.

That college perpetuates itself in fundamentalist churches all across the country. Graduates go back to those churches and tell people that skirts have to be below the knee, that sideburns can't be too long, and they pass it off as Christian behavior. That college and its graduates have tremendous clout among truly fundamentalist churches.

When my kids first went to their Christian college I was shocked to find out that the curfew was one a.m. In our college we were shepherded around because "the school owed it to the parents." We could only date with chaperones or in a dating parlor supervised by a monitor. It was true that you couldn't get into much trouble there, but you didn't learn to be responsible either.

I asked myself at first, *What guarantee do I have that my daughter will be okay without some strict rules?* Then I realized that the *only* guarantee that she has is God in her life. My son says that if a person is living a sinful life at college, he or she will be confronted by other believers, not just turned in to the authorities. Because they teach kids to be accountable to one another (which is really the biblical way), they are very open about confronting, counseling or just helping one another. But they confront in love—they don't just snitch. There's not that paranoid sense of having to follow the list for the sake of the school authorities.

When I was going off to college my pastor's wife took me aside and gave me some advice. She was a graduate and a real booster of our college too. She said, "Don't trust anyone at the school. Don't tell them anything. Keep everything to yourself."

How did you take that? Were you at all surprised or shocked?

I remember just accepting it. It seemed strange, but she was the pastor's wife—so I simply took note. You can see why we had such trouble opening up to others. Our congregation often fellowships with a church whose pastor went to that college, as well as many of the members. You can see the anger and fear they live under.

I think that we were actually taught not to love. Not directly, but indirectly. The liberals were always talking about love and the social gospel, so it was probably a reaction. It was almost as if our fundamentalist elders were saying, "We will preach the truth. To hell with love."

My father is still a militant fundamentalist, and he has a very hard time with love. One day my husband went down and painted Dad's little house while he was away. He just did it out of love, because my father is quite old now.

When Dad got back he was blown away. He didn't know how to respond, so he said, "What's he trying to do, go to heaven on his good works?" No kidding! That was all he could come up with.

My husband and I have agonized over this coldness and lack of humility in fundamentalism. Twenty-seven years after graduating from our college, we still have anguish because of it.

Now I can see that the isolation we lived in kept us from learning and growing. When we moved here we started associating with a wider range of Christians and saw that there were other ways to act. I'll never forget meeting Christians who could have a beer. How could this be? There were drinkers and there were Christians. You couldn't be both. Then we met Christians who didn't spank their kids. We were sure that Christians had to spank their kids to teach them discipline.

All our misunderstandings and misinterpretations of Scripture were validated by preachers. We had read that verse that says, "Be not drunk with wine, but be filled with the Holy Spirit." We had been taught that it meant that you could never, never, never, under any circumstance have a drink. But that's obviously not what it says. Besides, Jesus drank wine. But we would rationalize the veracity of our interpretation, and then the preachers would hammer it home. It was the same with verses about disciplining kids. We had never been taught to meditate on the Scriptures. We were taught what the Scriptures meant, and then it was reinforced again and again by our preachers.

Now I'm so ashamed of the stupid things I believed. We spanked too much, talked too little and never apologized to our kids. We kept hearing that spanking was our responsibility! We perpetuated it. We heard over and over that we needed to spank our kids, but who told us how to *love* them?

We heard a lot of meanness in the name of Christ. One preacher had a home for wayward girls. He came to our church to preach and told us about a girl who didn't like the oatmeal they served for breakfast. She was told, "Okay, you can have it for lunch." She got that same bowl of oatmeal for two weeks. We accepted it as a model of how to treat our kids. What mean, nasty thinking!

We spanked our boys for looking at us cross-eyed. Now they're talking about how to raise their kids. By the time our daughter came along we had begun to question the practice of spanking, so she got less of it. We were also beginning to learn about communicating love. And she has had far fewer problems.

I remember a woman at church asking me, "Do you yell at your kids? I feel bad that I yell at mine so much." I was the pastor's wife, and she was honestly asking my input. But our world was so isolated, I didn't have any real context to draw from.

I said, "Well, if that's what you have to do to get them to behave, I guess it's okay." I answered her from the context of that isolated little society. The bottom line was always to take the hard line. To soften, or question, was to go against God. "The Bible says it, so I believe it." But we never looked to see if that's what the Bible was really saying. What about the passage that tells us not to provoke our children to wrath?

We sat down with all three of our kids and apologized to them for the way we had raised them. We just admitted to them that we made some big mistakes. "We spanked you too much and didn't listen enough. We're sorry."

What else could we do? We were wrong, and we didn't want them to think that we still felt that we were right.

My father died recently, and my mother is now going back and sorting out her life. But when I talk to her she refuses to acknowledge that, like everyone, she made mistakes. I've had loving conversations with her, but if she feels backed into a corner she gets out the claws. She can't consider the *possibility* that she made any mistakes. It threatens her whole world.

Our old youth leader from California visited us a while ago, and he's the same way. He is retired now and still locked in that old fundamentalist mold. He brags about his perfect son who is a pastor, but he doesn't mention his divorced daughter and her three kids. The daughter doesn't consider herself a Christian, so he doesn't mention her.

When he and my husband went out, his wife opened up to me about marriage problems, family problems—the same things we all go through. She wants to admit mistakes and make changes, but he doesn't. If you question him, he just brags louder about his son and refuses to discuss the hurting daughter. He's stuck there, afraid to be honest.

My husband just resigned from his position, and we will probably go into some kind of mission work now. We have prayed about it a lot, and he feels strongly that he should be in a Christian ministry that doesn't put him in the role of pastor, where everything is on his shoulders. We received some very critical letters, which we expected, but we have peace about it.

Critical about leaving the pulpit to become a missionary? Why?

It seems that every move we make has to be second-guessed. They say things like "If you were out bringing people into your church you wouldn't have to jump ship." There's a certain amount of finger-pointing and guilt appeal.

That way of thinking goes on and on. My daughter is counseling at a summer camp. She was not home when the director called and left a message on the machine. He just said, "Remember. No shorts are permitted at the camp." Doesn't that just say it all? *She laughs sadly.* She's going off to counsel kids, share the gospel and teach. Some of those kids will come to camp with enormous family problems. There will be kids with divorcing parents, abusive homes—all the usual issues kids face. With all the monumental problems to think about, his big concern is that she might show up in short pants.

21

I Want to Be That Honest

Now in their middle thirties, John and Louise are married and have small children. They grew up in an affluent suburb of a large city, where their parents were among fourteen founding families of a small church. While they were in junior high school, the church attained social prominence.

Their parents and the parents of the other founding families are still very active in that church, where they are respected as spiritual and organizational role models by the rest of the congregation. John and Louise left the church in college when it was at the height of its popularity.

For several years they stayed out of church altogether; then they tried different congregations in other parts of the city. Recently they have returned, although they don't participate in the main worship service and avoid the social and political life of the church.

* * *

LOUISE: Our mothers are in a prayer and fellowship group that has been going on for many years. They get together and cry and pray about their kids who have all left the church. They had literally dozens of kids, and all but a handful are gone. Most of them aren't even Christians.

JOHN: They cry and pray, and pray and cry. *He laughs.* It's sad. Their kids rebelled, and they look for blame everywhere. They blame the schools, society . . .

LOUISE: They can't understand their kids' anger and rejection. It has never occurred to them that maybe they drove their kids out. I ran into some of the Reilly kids recently. There were seven of them growing up with us, mostly boys, and they're all gone. I tried to talk to them about my faith struggles, and they just said something like "You're pathetic. Don't talk to us about that Christ stuff. We have a new life now. That's old history!"

Their mother never missed a day of church in her life, and now her whole brood just laughs at her faith. But she still just keeps going to all her church activities and Bible studies, hoping that it will all work out somehow.

JOHN: It's sad. In that fellowship group they share what the Lord is doing in their life and ask for prayer, but they never talk about what's *really* happening in their lives. One lady was having an emotional breakdown, and for two years, while she was in treatment and taking medication, no one in that fellowship group knew a thing about it. When she finally broke down and was hospitalized, they were all shocked.

LOUISE: Another family was going bankrupt. Not a word was spoken about that! No sir! I said to my mother, "Her husband is making enemies because of the way he handles his business. Don't you guys ever discuss that?" She says, "Oh well, we wouldn't want to pry in their affairs."

It's maddening. My father, who is supposedly their friend, is an expert businessman who really understands finances. I asked him if they had ever asked for his input.

He said, "That's an interesting question." Another lady's husband was in rehab, but she hid it from the fellowship group.

No wonder their kids all left! Who would want to end up like that? Everything they do is for show, or, as they would say, a good witness. They put on the smiles and talk all the Christian talk, but a lot of them obviously can't stand their husbands. It's a sham.

My sister was in the young marrieds group. She and her husband were the perfect couple, but she started seeing what was going on. The young marrieds were in the same boat—fellowshipping, sharing and praying, but completely unaware of the divorces and other really big problems that some of the members were going through. She is starting to wonder what Christian fellowship is good for, now that she's seeing some of her friends' marriages fail. No one asks for help, because it would blow their cover.

JOHN: Their view of sin is that bad things are like a contagious disease. Bad things fall out of the sky and contaminate you. Their problems have nothing to do with the way they live their lives, although they would assign blame to people outside the church for *their* problems.

LOUISE: All that denial and covering up is a coping mechanism that gets passed on to the next generation. My cousin, whose family is also part of that group, died of AIDS. He hid his homosexuality from everyone for years. It was a compulsive behavior, which people in the church would be quick to condemn. But his compulsive behavior just manifested itself in a more unacceptable way. His father's compulsion (and my father's too) is his work, and our mothers' compulsion is their church activities. I believe that compulsive behavior is learned, because it's evident in all three generations of my family. I could see myself falling into it too.

Can you talk about that?

LOUISE: Well, I was into causes. I was saving the whales, saving the forests and working for prison reform and battered women. Those are all good causes, but I wasn't paying attention to John or our marriage. I was just going full-speed ahead on my crusades. I was becoming a version of my mother, just as my cousin became a version of his father.

John and I saw a marriage counselor, and he asked me why I didn't put some of my energy and passion into our marriage. Then we had kids, and I really saw what he meant. I'm geared to run fast and not stop to let anyone touch me.

My cousin who died of AIDS was very much like me in that way. He was the life of the party and a real cut-up. In school he was the social center of everything. He would have these intense experiences with people and they would think that he was their best friend; then they wouldn't see him for a year. He couldn't stand it when he got close enough to be real. He liked to blast into your life and then split. His sexual compulsion was that way too.

Most fundamentalists would have a hard time accepting a link between promiscuous sex and overcommitment at church or work.

JOHN: It's the same thing. Our folks were always busy in church, always up front. They were the deacons and the teachers, but they couldn't ever admit a mistake. They couldn't let anyone know that they had doubts about anything. I think they just buried themselves in church as a way of hiding from the real issues in their lives.

They don't have any friends. They have acquaintances, but not friends. Having friends would require being open and vulnerable. They would have to drop the veil.

LOUISE: Their version of the gospel promised so much. They couldn't admit, even to themselves, that it wasn't delivering.

What promises did it not deliver?

LOUISE: My mother was always telling me to order my life around God's will. If I didn't I would miss all the fulfillment. But

I looked at my parents, and they sure didn't seem fulfilled. Our parents don't show affection toward one another or to their kids.

My mother can't stand her own mother. Grandma is very active, or at least she has been until quite recently. But Grandma can't stand my mother and always complains about her. She doesn't like being around the grandchildren or the great-grandchildren. She's always afraid our kids will make noise or spill something. And she criticizes constantly.

My father is like a robot. He's very wealthy and successful, but he can't hug his kids. He can only work. He was gone much of the time, and when he was at home we were always afraid we would make him upset.

What you are describing is fairly common in modern families. Probably half the people in the country would relate a similar story. Is it really a fault of fundamentalist teaching? Isn't it just plain old family dysfunction?

JOHN: That's true, but our folks always had the weight of God's Word behind their actions. They would read James Dobson's books, go to Bill Gothard's seminars, teach classes, and there would always be this great promise of the fulfill ing Christian life. But you're right. It was the same dysfunctional family style that you could get without God. So why believe?

I used to have a huge anger problem. I still do, but I work on it. I spent several years on drugs, and I know that a lot of my addiction was just a way to tune out of the crazy family situation.

I'm not saying that our parents are terrible monsters, but they speak with God's authority, and deep down they're needy people who need to listen and learn. My father has the emotional level of a five-year-old. If you changed his voice he would sound just like a small child. I criticized him about something minor, and he blew up: "What about *you?"* I shouldn't have laughed, but I did.

I know that I have to own my own rebellion. Those years of drugs and crazy behavior were my choice. That's the bottom line. But kids don't rebel against nothing. Why are all the kids from those fourteen families gone? Why did so many of them rebel?

Louise and I have seen family counselors about this, because we want the cycle to stop with us. Our parents and their parents screwed up, and then they tried to tell us that everything they did was part of God's big plan. I say no to that. I want my parents to own their mistakes so we can grow through this together.

LOUISE: John had a particularly violent outburst when our kids were little, and that's when we just said, "Hey, we have to get some help on this."

JOHN: I was at my folks' place, and my father said something that really set me off. I was cursing and destroying furniture. I said, "You aren't listening!" He said, "What do you mean?" We were completely unable to communicate. My rage was uncontrollable and very ugly. I could see how people end up in jail. I was beating up the furniture, but it could have been my wife or kids or whoever was unlucky enough to be there.

LOUISE: We had gone to a premarital counselor, and he actually warned us about all of this in advance. He could see very clearly back then, and he didn't even know our families. We chose a counselor from another church because we didn't want to go to our parents' pastor. We said, "Yeah, yeah, we've heard all this." He said, "No, you haven't." He was using Bible terms that we used all the time, about love and forgiveness and humility, but he was right. We didn't have a clue about what any of it meant because we had lived in a world of denial and appearances.

JOHN: We come from families who don't know how to ask for help. They have to appear like they're in charge. They would say that they are just trying to present a good witness. If you live like that for a while, you begin to believe it.

I read that communication is 7 percent verbal and 93 percent nonverbal. Our parents' religion stressed the *appearance* of perfection, so they worked very hard on the 7 percent. They said all the right things. But their kids grew up to be angry, alienated people, many of whom engage in dangerous behavior.

I know what I'm capable of. I've had to own my anger and my drug use. I want to stop the cycle, but I don't believe that simply moving away and pretending that I don't have a family history will help. I want my family to join me in the healing process—for everyone's sake.

I started reading the Bible again, and I was shocked at the problems David, Jacob, Abraham and all those guys had. They were major screw-ups, but they asked for forgiveness. In the fundamentalist church you have to keep everything hidden, so you can't ask for forgiveness. You would have to admit failure.

The gospel we heard promised us that the big sins would be for other people. But the truth is that we have seen adultery, drunkenness, drug abuse, homosexuality and many other problems. Just like in the Bible.

LOUISE: Yeah. The same Bible that they thump every week. It's all in there. I still marvel at the way you can read the Bible and come up with the idea that we will all be able to live perfect lives if we just don't say anything.

I try to talk to my mother about this *(she sighs),* but she doesn't get it. She actually asked me once, "What's all this *forgiveness* talk?" If you read the Bible, it should be fairly clear where all the forgiveness talk comes from.

I have an aunt who lives the perfect life. She's really busy in her church, and everything has to be exactly right. She actually said once, "I can't help it if we're better than

95 percent of the people out there." If that's true, who needs Jesus?

JOHN: That attitude rubs off on you. Once my mother had to come to school when I was in trouble for an impulsive prank that caused some damage. We spent two hours with the principal, but I never apologized. I knew that I had done something wrong, but it didn't occur to me to apologize. When we left she was steaming. "You could have just apologized!" she said. But I had never seen that modeled. Any talk about sin ("the S-word") was always vague. No one ever owned up to doing anything wrong. When did my parents ever apologize for anything? A kid doesn't just figure out how to repent all by himself.

That's why none of those fourteen families can imagine that they might have done anything to mess up their kids. When their kids turn out bad, it doesn't occur to them to ask why.

LOUISE: I see my brother-in-law becoming like my parents, and the strain is starting to show up in his kids like it did with me. I asked him to think about his own sin, but the only thing he could come up with was that once he ran in the hall when he was in school. Talk about denial! But I was the same way. I didn't understand the tremendous pride and arrogance that I was guilty of.

My brother-in-law has a lot to lose by looking at sin from a biblical perspective. His whole life has revolved around not causing conflict. He has fooled himself about his own heart.

We see friends' marriages fail, and the dumpee invariably says something like, "He's not the guy I married." Well, yes he is. If you think someone is perfect, you won't ever expect anything from them. If your marriage fails, it probably has something to do with you. It's never the fault of one person.

My parents, as well as my aunt and uncle, are starting

to see the writing on the wall. They could end up alone and disillusioned, but they won't talk to one another except on the most superficial level. My aunt won't confront my uncle about the hurt she has suffered because of him. She says, "Well, he has a good job and he's a good husband." Sure, but he doesn't talk to her about my cousin's death or the fact that they can't communicate with their kids. He treats her like a maid.

My cousin knew when he was dying that he had made bad choices, but he also knew, toward the end, that his family had a lot to do with the way he was. I think a part of my anger is that if his parents had been able to say, "We're partly to blame," he could have said, "No, I'm to blame." But his folks just couldn't admit any wrong.

And my cousin, even though he grew in his faith after he got sick, was still locked into the need to make appearances. Sometimes he would want to bolt when he got too close or too honest with me. We were about the same age, and we were very close growing up.

Some people are going to read this and wonder why you don't just get on with your own life and leave your parents and their generation to their own devices.

LOUISE: I think about that too. But my children come from a family. My father is changing very slowly. Our daughter is a very open and loving kid, and when she sees him she runs up to him and embraces him. He responds to that, and it's beautiful to see. He carries her around the house and talks to her. I want that for him, and for my mother.

But my mother has a lot to lose. Why rock the boat? She has money, time and full reign over the house. She can stay busy at church and have lots of fellowship without ever being honest and putting herself at risk. I think she's afraid of what she would find out if she really opened herself up.

John and I have been going to church—well, to Sunday school anyway—for the last year or two. We searched around, but we found that the problems in our church are present everywhere to some extent. We feel—I never thought I would talk like this—sort of *called* to come back and put in our time.

JOHN: We finally stopped bitching and moaning about the superficial classes and started our own class. The church has gotten a lot smaller in recent years, but there are some people in our age group—people with young kids—who are coming back.

Tell me about your class.

JOHN: We just try to meet needs. We don't do the verse study thing that they would prefer, like a study of Genesis or something. We've had people come in and talk about discipline versus punishment. We even had a CPR class. We're trying to deal with real needs.

A lot is changing with our generation. I think, for instance, that men are beginning to wake up and take stock. A lot of guys my age don't want to be like their fathers, but we still fall into the same thinking if we don't work at changing.

For instance, we got on the subject of sin, and we ended up discussing sexual addiction, pornography and so on. These are real problems for some people, but I said that my problem with anger is just as big of a problem. At first everyone was telling me that it wasn't, but I insisted that it was. The porno stuff is one of those "out there" sins. Either it's not a problem for us personally, or we wouldn't admit it if it was. But my anger has caused huge problems with my parents, my sister and my wife. It's a result of real sin.

My feeling (and this is true for some but not all of the other guys) is that I want to be honest and own up to my problems. The Bible says that perfect love casts out fear. Our parents and those other families are afraid. Now they are victims of their own fear.

Your pastor is quite well known. He's one of the first-string clergy-

men in this city. Did you ever talk to him about your frustrations with the church?

JOHN: You know what? I never did. I hate to say it, but his family is one of the families I'm talking about. He's a dynamic preacher and a great organizer, but he was never interested in getting intimate and honest. At least not that we could see.

Our youth pastor was more of a Young Life kind of guy. He was great at getting kids to come out for activities and getting them to accept Christ, but he was not interested in the real, day-to-day issues that we have been talking about.

You have probably seen other churches like ours. There's a lot of money there, and I actually had one deacon tell me that God had blessed us because we were good people. The members have beautiful homes and great cars, and they take fantastic vacations. I think it's easy to feel that things are going well when you're affluent. If you're poor you might wonder if you had screwed up and think that your condition is God's wrath, but that's harder to do when you have everything you want.

There was a lot going on in the church as we grew up. Lots of evangelism, outreach programs and good preaching. Some of the professional athletes were very active there, and it was just the happening place to be. It's very prestigious to have an all-star pitcher or center teaching your Sunday-school class. It must have been easy to think that everything was going great.

My mother was counseling a young woman. *He laughs and shakes his head.* If you knew my mother you would understand why that is so funny. Anyway, this woman was sharing her burdens, and my mother just shook her head and said, "Wow! You *do* have problems!" She didn't know what to tell the woman. Not a clue. She couldn't just suffer with her. She looked at her like she was a freak with a horrible disease.

I want to break out of that kind of thinking. I know that I have messed my life up. I wrote a letter to my sister, apologizing for my behavior when I was on drugs all those years. She wrote back saying she that forgave me, then spent five pages spilling her bile. She ended it with "God bless you." Later when I talked to her about it, she couldn't understand why I had considered her letter an angry one. But I deserved her anger. I wasn't a brother to her, and I wasn't a son to my parents. I admit it. It's hard to admit it, but it's true. I made my parents afraid of me, and I have to live with that. I have to work to make it better. I just wish my sister could admit that she's angry too, so we could move on. She can be angry, but why not admit it? I guess she says she isn't angry because Christians aren't supposed to hold on to their anger.

Louise's cousin, the guy who died of AIDS, said once that if his parents ever took stock of all the slights, insults, snubs and cruelties they had inflicted on one another over the forty years of their marriage—if they both did it at the same time on the same day—they would kill one another.

I learned a lot from him. Once, not too long before he died, we had a great time sharing and talking. I thought, *Boy, he's really got it together!* Then he said that he had been in a gay bar earlier that evening picking up guys. That blew me away. But he said he knew he was wrong and that he was forgiven. He wasn't proud of what he had done, and he didn't want to do it again, but he admitted it to me. He didn't want to have little secrets or put up a front anymore.

I want to be that honest. I want to be forgiven and know it. Then I can change and grow in the Lord. It pains me to see my parents and their friends getting more self-centered and closed to the possibility of forgiveness and growth in the Lord. I don't want to grow old and find out that I didn't know my kids.

You can't know true forgiveness until you drop the

pretense and admit that you are who you are. When you admit what you are and what you have done, maybe you can finally have the Christian life that they are trying so hard to pretend they have.

22

Grace Breaks the Cycle of Abuse

She's a professional counselor in her forties, a wife and the mother of grown children. I get the impression that she would feel perfectly comfortable meeting the president or addressing a huge crowd. She comes across as very competent and professional, yet she has the easy manner of a next-door neighbor sharing a cup of coffee.

She's well groomed but not flashy. She's hard to peg. She could be a lawyer, a pastor or a stay-at-home mother.

We first meet at a gathering of mutual friends, where we immediately strike up a long conversation on the topic of child abuse in Christian families.

* * *

I was severely abused as a child. When I was five, my father beat me so badly that I ended up in the hospital. The nurse asked me how I got all the bruises and welts on my body. I remember saying, "I was naughty, so Daddy spanked me." I was twenty-four when I realized that I had been abused. Until then I had just accepted it as the way things were. That's understandable in a five-year-old, but that nurse must have known that it was wrong for a child to be beaten up like that, yet she didn't say anything.

I accepted Jesus at a Bible camp the summer before eighth grade, along with my sister. Our family wasn't Christian then, but the following summer my dad was saved, and we all joined a strict fundamentalist church. We breathed easier for a while because my father changed somewhat, but soon the abuse resumed. The last real beating had been when I was eight years old, but the verbal and psychological abuse continues until this day.

Church wasn't much help, but we were in a little Christian school, and that was my salvation (not my actual salvation). I was accepted there, and one teacher in particular treated me like a real person.

The kids in my class were very accepting too. My sister's class was a different story, but I felt that my classmates accepted me. They were more affluent than I was, but that wasn't the center of their lives, so it wasn't really an obstacle.

My father only had a fourth-grade education. He was pulled out of school to work on the farm. They were sharecroppers, and he just didn't have much to fall back on, emotionally or intellectually. His parents abused him terribly, so he was just repeating what he knew.

We had the oldest house in a fairly well-to-do neighborhood. I think the structure was valued at about two thousand dollars. He had me paint the house one year, and I had to work hard and fast to try to please him. I would come home from school and get right to work. I hated it when the school bus went past. I wasn't ashamed of having to paint the house, but I just felt that everyone could see my overall fear and shame. In my mind the shabbiness of our house, my father's lack of education and the abuse were all tied together. My classmates' families and homes seemed quite different, and I couldn't imagine them being physically and emotionally abused like I was.

I was so busy painting that I didn't complete a major term paper in one class. The teacher called me in privately and asked in a very kind way, "Does this have to do with your painting job?" I blushed with shame and said that it did. He simply told me, "Well, don't worry about it. Just turn it in when you can." He trusted my integrity and took my word. It felt like God. He didn't remove me from the home like they would today, but I felt that he understood. He came alongside and walked with me.

I read the Bible and didn't really find any inconsistency in it. The inconsistency was in my father and the church. When that teacher treated me with kindness, it felt like the God I read about in the Bible.

One time he took me to his vacation cabin. His daughter and I were friends. That week was the only time in my life that I hadn't lived in fear for my life. Again, it felt like God.

I used to think that I would never leave my home alive. I believed that if I tried, my dad would go berserk and kill me—literally. I believed that he would just get his gun and murder the whole family. But I felt that if I ever *did* get away, I would be safe if I got to that teacher's house.

He performed our marriage ceremony. My father wanted our pastor to do it, but I wanted my marriage to start out with God's blessing. We compromised and let the pastor offer a prayer. The teacher, who was also a pastor, did something that surprised me. He prayed for the children we would have, which was something I had never even considered. It just opened up a possibility I hadn't considered.

Do you think that by praying for children in your home he was acknowledging to you that he understood what you had suffered?

You know, I had never thought of it that way until you said it just now, but that's probably true. I'll ask him. To this day he is the strongest male figure in my life.

Not all the teachers were that way, though. Once a teacher came into class and, in front of all the other students, asked me, "Is your dad crazy or something?" Well, the truth is that my father was mentally ill. Severely disturbed. What brought on the teacher's question was my father's response in a PTA meeting the night before. Some of us in the choir had performed at a county fair. We wore uniforms at that school, but we were in street clothes at the fair. My father saw us, and I had my hair in bangs. For some reason he felt that only whores wore bangs.

Anyway, he stood up at the PTA meeting and yelled, "My daughter is a whore. She was wearing a short skirt and bangs!" The teacher repeated that to the class. I felt like dying. I don't think that he had any idea what he had done to me by repeating my father's condemnation.

My husband came from a similar family with lots of severe abuse. Our fathers were both well respected in their churches. In fact, my father was made chairman of the board almost immediately. I remember him going down to buy Roberts's *Rules of Order* so he could run the meetings properly. It was pathetic, really. He was so excited about being in charge. It was probably that excitement and enthusiasm that led the church to put him in charge like that.

It's strange how the pull of that kind of church has a hold on you. My husband and I continued going to churches like that until very recently. Our last church was horribly dysfunctional.

What led you to get out of that brand of strict fundamentalism?

My introduction to therapy and psychology. When my daughter was five she was sexually abused by my husband's father. We knew right away that something was wrong. Five-year-olds don't usually talk about killing themselves. At first the church wanted to deal with it internally. My husband's father was the Sunday-school superintendent and well respected in the church. We must have spent six months dithering around with deacons and elders before I just took it to the top. I got no hearing from the pastor or deacons, so I went to the association to get him removed from his post. I explained that it wasn't to punish him, but to protect other children. They removed him, but they never really understood. It was just an attempt to quiet things down.

The man is a pedophile, and it turns out that he's had about a hundred victims. He wouldn't get counseling, though. Now he's a foreign missionary.

That's when I started studying psychology. I did a research project on three fundamentalist churches, using Kohlberg's stages of moral reasoning as a model. Kohlberg identified six stages of moral reasoning that are sequential, but not necessarily chronological. In other words, some young people reason at a high moral level, while some adults function morally as though they were children.

The highest stage is rare. Only a few people reach it, like Mother Teresa, who does everything for a purpose much larger than herself, or a martyr who dies rather than going along with evil.

Most people function around stage four. I don't remember the exact definitions now. But in those churches I found that the adults were all functioning at a level two or three. Actually, the men functioned at two and the women at three. Those churches are populated and managed by extremely immature people. My father is in his sixties, but, as I said before, he has the emotional maturity of a five-year-old.

When I finally saw this I thought, *Praise God! I'm not crazy. It's not me that needs to grow up!* I'm not saying that I'm perfect, of course. But it was a great relief to finally understand why these people could read the Bible and then look the other way while men beat their wives and children, or why they were so legalistic.

Like small children, they follow rules out of fear of punishment. They don't love God's law, or even understand it. They just want to keep out of trouble. If God's punishment doesn't come, they will make it happen. There's no understanding of God's grace.

How do you mean?

Sin has logical consequences. On a very basic level, promiscuous sex, for instance, can lead to pregnancy or disease. But if someone is sinning and they don't seem to be having a miserable time, fundamentalists will add their own punishments just to make sure. There's too much condemnation. They treat one another like children on the playground, except there is no adult to make them get along, because the more mature people leave or are forced out.

One of my subjects suggested that theology is often just personality types looking for justification.

Exactly! That's why there are so many authoritarian males like my father. They are very immature men who have to be in charge, so they add rules to God's law.

Any responsible adult in that church could have seen the abuse in my family, and in my husband's family. But there weren't any responsible adults *in* those churches. They had all left.

When I set out on my research project I fully expected to find that people were operating at stage four or five. I still consider myself a fundamentalist, and I believe in God's power to make us new. It was extremely disappointing, but also very enlightening, to see, in a quantifiable way, the low level of maturity among the leadership of the churches.

Getting back to the idea that theology is personality types looking for justification, I think he has something there, but I think that true theology is psychology.

That's a very unusual statement for a fundamentalist to make. Most fundamentalists are very distrustful of psychology.

I was too. As a young person I was fascinated by it, but I didn't delve too deeply because I was afraid (I realize now) of what I might find. I think I knew that if I really examined the hard-core fundamentalism of my church, I would see my belief structure fall apart.

But that doesn't seem to have happened.

Not at all. Psychology helps people put the three parts of human experience together: body, soul and spirit. They aren't really separate. We have just made them that way. So, yes, much of the fundamentalist mindset is exposed as heresy if you examine it, but not Christianity.

In fairness to those churches, I think that some of the fundamentalist preachers have a real gift of evangelism. They are gifted in bringing people to Christ, even though they are operating at a very immature level. But once people grow to adolescence, which requires a higher level of moral reasoning where they are able to ask questions, they become a threat. You have to ask questions if you expect to gain moral wisdom, but asking is too scary. If you don't fall in line, you are put under judgment. Some people, like me, move on to something similar. When you finally grow, you move to a higher level.

The problem is that people who are operating at a higher level of moral reasoning can coexist with those operating at a lower level. It's just like adults and children. A mature adult isn't threatened by a child, although she might get frustrated by that child.

But adults who are functioning as children are threatened by mature thinkers. Very threatened. They don't understand, and they equate the higher level of reasoning with heresy.

That study helped me to understand why I kept going to those churches, and why I kept getting into so much trouble. Now I can thank God that I'm growing and not feel that there's something wrong with me. Real maturity allows you to move up. You don't have to be mad at God and rebel. But if there's no structure for you to mature, you may end up rebelling against all authority.

I was driving once and saw a mother pulled over by the side of the road, hitting her child. I pulled over and asked, "Can I be of help?" I didn't just pass by, which is what people did when I was being beaten up. She wasn't really abusing the child—it looked worse than it was—but I had to be sure.

However, I was working in a hospital one time and I saw a parent really abusing a child. She was hitting him over the head with a rolled magazine. I called security, and the guard said it was no big deal. We got into a big argument, and he said, "I've been a cop for twenty years and I know abuse." I replied that I had been abused and that I was also a counselor. I told him people like him were the problem. I was very rude to him, embarrassing him in public. So he filed a complaint.

I apologized for swearing at him and losing my temper, which was wrong, but I didn't back down on the issue of abuse. I was still going through my own therapy, so my anger was immature. Now I've done my work on my abuse, and I don't think I would treat him that way again.

You have to get to the point where you realize what a fallen world we live in and accept that often there's no good solution. Had I been pulled from my home and placed in foster care, there's a very strong probability that I would have been sexually abused. You can't fix everything, but you have to do what God calls you to do. That's why I respect that teacher who walked alongside me back in my Christian-school days. He didn't turn a blind eye, but he didn't think he was going to charge in and fix it either.

You said earlier that you kept getting in trouble in your churches.

Can you give an example of the kind of trouble you're talking about?

I was kicked out of my last church, where my husband was one of several associate pastors. The head pastor was an extremely gifted evangelist who started the church in a house and saw it grow, in the course of a decade, to several thousand members. But he was an authoritarian leader who drove people out.

I saw thirty-two couples come to Christ in that church and then leave or get ostracized. In almost every case the wife was a victim of sexual or physical abuse. That was the common thread.

I was going back over my own life and doing therapy, so I noticed this and decided to study it. That's when I did the study on Kohlberg's stages of moral reasoning. I saw that our church was a perfect model of a dysfunctional family. The minister was the abusive father, and the deacons were like siblings. One elder, a man my husband and I brought into the church, was acting like the mother. He loved the minister because he had come to Christ under his preaching and teaching, but he was always running interference between the minister and the people who were like abused children.

There was also misuse of funds that had been given when the church had joined a larger denomination. This was quite obvious, but pastoral staff members and lay leaders covered for the minister, just like in a dysfunctional family. The minister was kicking the kids out of the house for rebelliousness, which was really just their adolescent stage of Christian growth. As they grew they had questions.

My husband had been in an auto wreck and was very vulnerable at the time, so he wasn't in a position to do much. He was sick and partly paralyzed. He had brought up the funds issue, so he was on his way out. The elder had tried to intervene, but it was like an abusive husband and a long-suffering wife. When the wife stands up for the kids, she gets beaten up or kicked out.

The church was in sad shape with so many hurt people being driven out. All the good work was being overshadowed by the authoritarianism.

By that time I had finished my research project on the stages of moral reasoning. The elder, in desperation, asked me to share it with the minister.

I said that I would, but only if all the elders were present. I stated very firmly that I would not deal with the minister one-on-one. It was several months before they could all be together on the same night.

By then the minister forbade me to sing in the church as a way of keeping me under his control.

Why? What kind of songs were you singing?

A song called "El Shaddai." I heard the song and was moved by it. It was simple and in my range, and I felt that it would be part of my healing to get up in front of people and share a song. It was well received. A terminally ill woman even told the elder she had walked into the service and accepted Christ. But that was the only solo I ever sang. I wasn't planning to sing publicly again. But the ban was not just solos, you understand. I was not allowed to sing in the pews. It was a test of my submission.

You're kidding. You mean you couldn't sing out of the hymnbook with the rest of the congregation?

Right. I was told to sit silently. I really think the minister was paranoid and wanted to neutralize me. Of course it wasn't as though God couldn't hear me singing along in my mind. Then the minister ordered me to write an essay on submission.

This is strange. You were an adult wife of an associate pastor and a trained counselor at that time, weren't you? Most people would have just walked at that point.

I'm sure that's what he wanted me to do, but I didn't want to continue being the victim. And much of the problem in our fundamentalist churches is directly the result of the authoritarian men we allow to run them. We give almost unlimited power to very insecure, immature men, and they drive people away. It's almost like we get what we deserve.

We met, and I presented the study and my essay on submission. Because of my abusive background I had a problem with the word *submission,* which men use as a club on women and kids in those churches. I used the word *deference* instead, although now I am past the problem with semantics.

None of the elders could see a problem, but the minister shook the manuscript and said, "This is heresy!" He wanted to haul me up in front of the congregation the next Sunday and excommunicate me. He actually said, "They used to burn people at the stake for trash like this!"

He had just excommunicated a woman for not submitting to her husband, who was the choir director. The man was a coke addict and he was beating her. It was really beyond dysfunction at this point. I know you're wondering why I didn't run, but remember, there were several thousand church members, many of whom were new Christians. I wanted to do what I could. If the whole thing just fell apart, it would hurt a lot of good people.

None of the elders had a problem with what I had written, but, under pressure, most of them voted me out. The elder who had been acting as the mother stood up and said, "This won't happen while I'm an elder here." He was removed and replaced with an alcoholic military man. The others who disagreed were all replaced as well, and the new elders voted me out, so it was unanimous. The whole episode was all about power and control. It had nothing to do with the gospel.

You seem at peace about this. I would expect you to be ranting and raving, or crying. You just have this calm Mona Lisa smile. What gives?

I think I understand what was going on, and I don't hate those people. I feel sorry for them, but I understand now how they get locked in that mode.

The national body was trying to disassociate itself from that church, but their bylaws made it impossible. One of the national representatives read my study and asked, "Why do you remain there? We need you and your understanding in our churches." My paper was fine, but not for people operating at level two. That's all.

That church has split three times, and there's a trail of hurt and brokenness, but I know that I tried to be faithful. I didn't want my children to get the idea that you just run from one bad situation to another. That is too often the model of relationships in society. I was hoping that we might break through and be able to grow, even though I knew it was unlikely. But we're not called to produce results, only to be faithful to God's Word. I tried to do that. I didn't want to keep living as though I was under my father's abusive rule, where I just had to cringe in fear all the time.

Did you ever achieve a breakthrough with your father?

Yes. He was having bypass surgery, so I drove up to Chicago from our home in Indiana to be with him. I didn't want to go, because it was a life-threatening situation and I was afraid that he would die and my last memory of him would be him yelling at me and berating me.

I did go, and it was tense and unpleasant. But my sister hadn't spoken to him for fifteen years, and my mother had died, so I was all he had. After a few days he was stable, so that evening I said I was going home to be with the kids and would come back soon.

He blew up at me and said, "You're crazy to drive at night! What's the matter with you?" He always told me I was crazy. Then he had chest pains, and the monitors started flashing and beeping. The crisis unit came in and worked on him, so I stayed the night.

The next day, when he came to, I went in and he asked me, in a soft way, "Do you think that was caused by stress?"

Well, he had never asked my opinion on anything before, and I knew those words weren't part of his vocabulary. Obviously he had gotten really frightened and had actually listened to the doctor. I said, "Yes, Daddy. Stress can cause a lot of physical problems."

Then the breakthrough came. He said, "Well, I worry about you driving back to Indiana at night. It's dangerous."

I realized then that he was saying the same thing he had said the night before, but in a different way. He was concerned about me.

I wish I could say it's all better now, just like a TV movie. He's still very abusive, but at least he's aware of it to some degree and tries to be nicer. I understand that he's such a limited, hurt and abused person that he doesn't have the skills to do much more than he's doing. He even thought about moving in with me and my family. I couldn't believe that. He was so moved by our ability to be intimate that he was like a little boy. It was very sad to see.

He didn't, though. He's not in a church right now. He finds a new church where he thinks the pastor is God, then he eventually has a fight over something and leaves. There's only so many churches like that, and he's using them up. He's pretty lonely.

Tell me about your new church.

It's very different. Our motto is "Growing together to become more like Jesus." There's a real sense that none of us has arrived. It's a very conservative church that you could probably call fundamentalist, but the whole tone is different.

We had a couple living in adultery. They had lay positions in the church, and it was quite hurtful. But the deacons went to them privately and urged them to repent. When they indicated that they had no desire to stop living in adultery, they were excommunicated.

The difference was enormous, though. The pastor told the congregation, but he didn't go into details. It was presented lovingly and with an open invitation to return. It felt like God. I cried when I realized how different it could be. I'm so happy to be out of that oppressive system and in a church like this one.

How did your own children deal with all this turmoil?

They're not perfect, of course. Our daughter is in her twenties now, and the long-term effects of sexual abuse have taken their toll. Like many victims, she had to deal with a lot of sexual confusion. She's a Christian, but she's tentative.

I think that in our last church I was very focused on the needs of the congregation and my own growth, but maybe I didn't realize how powerful a spectacle it was for our kids. I trust that they will benefit in the long run, but maybe we should have left sooner. I just don't know.

I can see that after all I have been through, God has blessed me and helped me to grow. I like who I am now, and I would be happy to meet more people like me.

I took great comfort from the Old Testament when I was growing up. People like Abigail, Esther, Joseph and Caleb were real examples for me of the way God works and is not bound by what we think are the rules.

When Esther was taken to be the king's concubine, she was really just going to be a whore. That's what we would call it today. She must have been crushed as a young girl to be put in that position. All the women of Israel dreamed of becoming the mother of the Messiah, and as the pagan king's whore that put her out of the running. But she saved her people. She couldn't possibly have known it would turn out that way.

After the battle of Jericho, Caleb took Rahab the harlot, another whore, as his wife. Yet Christ came from that line. Boaz broke the law by marring Ruth, and again it led to Christ.

Even as a young girl I saw a consistency in the Bible. God was bigger than the rules. He even seemed to break his own rules. I didn't have to come from a perfect Christian family. I had horrible examples, yet God has blessed me and given me insights to help others that I might not have gotten otherwise. God's grace can help us break the cycles of misery and abuse.

Using that line of thinking, even your father's conversion and church activities have led to something positive. You probably couldn't have imagined that.

No. I had an abusive father who was from an even more abusive home. He became a fundamentalist Christian. But what if I'd just had an abusive father? It's taken time, but my father and I are talking now. My kids are seeing that the cycle doesn't have to go on forever.

Afterword

In conducting the interviews for this book I was struck with the thought that my subjects could be roughly divided into two groups. No human being can truly know another's deepest heart, and it would be pointless to categorize individuals rigidly, but it seemed that one group had encountered a religion while the other had encountered Christ. That is what seemed to determine the nature of each person's spiritual journey.

Those who found religion had been successfully inoculated and felt no need to examine Scripture or the claims of Christ. Their spiritual journey led them toward human solutions to life's great problems and mysteries. Those who had encountered Christ walked a difficult road, struggling mightily to separate dogma, fairy tales, political biases and ethnocentrism from the historical Jesus.

Many of the baby boomers who fled or just drifted away from Christianity in the sixties began to return when they had children of their own. Some returned to find the risen Christ, or to become reacquainted. Others returned for structure and support. Many more returned because of the negative influences they saw eroding their ability to raise decent, honest children. Shocked by the power of the popular culture to shape their children's values, they launched a counteroffensive.

What will the children of the baby boomers have to say about *their* upbringing a generation from now, when they hit middle age? Will someone write a book called *Surviving a Megachurch and Its Many Programs,* or *I Was a Teenage Codependent Inner Child?* What lazy thinking, smug arrogance or willful denial will shape their questioning and rebellion?

A final metaphor might be helpful. Albert E. Greene of Alta Vista College explains true spiritual freedom with the metaphor of a river. A river is constantly in flux. It swells with the rains and snowmelts and recedes with the summer sun. Anyone who has rafted one of the great rivers knows that it changes constantly. It can run still and deep one moment, then narrow to a raging, frothing torrent as it shoots through a tight canyon. It can plummet hundreds of feet in a cascading waterfall or drift through reedy wetlands. But it is a river only as long as it is contained within its banks. It is only *free* to be a river when contained within its banks.

If a river escapes its banks, it's not really a river anymore. It's hardly free. It's just a chaotic, destructive flood that eventually becomes a puddle, then dries up completely. That's what happens when human beings rebel and forget that they are meant to live within the banks of God's Word.

But God's Word isn't like a water pipe. A pipe is unnaturally confining. The water in it always goes in exactly the same direction. It flows along without rapids, eddies, swimming pools or fishing holes. It flows in the dark. When it gets where it's going, it can serve a useful purpose, like irrigating crops or flushing the toilet, and we can appreciate it for that, but not in the same way we appreciate the Frazer River as it roars through Hell's Gate in British Columbia, or the Snake as it winds through Idaho forests and canyons. A pipe for water is a human invention. It lacks the majesty of God's hand.

The church of Jesus Christ is always one generation from extinction, and adults must always remember that they are preparing the young to carry on. But as the young navigate through life they must be like rivers. Not floods. Not pipes.

If they are left to their own devices they run the risk of overflowing their banks and—like the Mississippi swollen by runoff from clearcuts and parking lots—wreaking havoc. But if they are forced into pipes, so that their every movement can be controlled by the valves and couplings of dogma, they will never know what it is to be a river. They will never know what it is to be as God made them—beautiful, wild, majestic and full of surprises.